Under a Broad Sky

ALSO BY RONALD BLYTHE

UNDER A BROAD SKY

RONALD BLYTHE

CANTERBURY
PRESS
Norwich

© Ronald Blythe 2013

First published in 2013 by the Canterbury Press Norwich
Editorial office
3rd Floor, Invicta House,
108–114 Golden Lane,
London EC1Y 0TG.

Canterbury Press is an imprint of Hymns Ancient & Modern Ltd
(a registered charity)
13A Hellesdon Park Road, Norwich,
Norfolk, NR6 5DR, UK

www.canterburypress.co.uk

British Library Cataloguing in Publication data

A catalogue record for this book is available
from the British Library

ISBN 978 1 84825 474 9

Printed and bound in Sweden by
ScandBook AB

For Frances Ward

Contents

Contents

Under a Broad Sky

JANUARY

Thawing Out

IT IS a relief to find that one does not gain a mature vision of everything – that the first sight of snow, for example, will be as serviceable, wonder-wise, as that of all the snowfalls in one's life. A six-inch snowfall establishes a presidency that takes our breath away, partly by its nerve, partly by its loveliness, bringing our ant movements to a halt, transforming everything from twig to a cathedral. There are no permanent snowfields in this country, so that even the white tops of the Welsh and Scottish mountains are ephemeral, year-lasting though they may appear.

As children, we would hang on to our snow. A patch in a ditch would tantalizingly last for a week or two after a thaw. We would visit it and tell it to hang on. Or our snowman would melt to a kind of licked lolly, his pipe slipped away, his face dripping and eyeless, yet still greyly what we had made him seemingly ages ago; and he, too, was urged to endure.

Snow is water vapour that has been frozen at a high altitude into exquisite crystals that are precipitated on to the earth, like rain, by gravity. The pattern of each snow crystal is endlessly various and beautiful beyond description. Snow is autocratic, commanding its own silence, bringing our world to a halt. Yet such is our disbelief in its rule, from

Mr Woodhouse in *Emma* to the Channel Tunnellers, that we set out when it begins to fall. Naturally, his carriage will be in trouble from it, but our carriages?

House-sized trucks swing this way and that on the motorway. One of life's little luxuries is to watch the world sliding about on a television screen, the fire blazing, the snow enthroned for as far as one can see, and those who think that they can beat it in a rare old muddle.

It drifted into my farm-track, and Henry the Vicar saw Jamie the postman gallantly stumbling through it with my letters. The horses wore their snow blankets and steamed in groups; the blackbirds fed on a square of swept grass; the oaks and ashes groaned and creaked; the churchwardens considered cancellations; and the snow snowed and snowed.

The forecasts were as black as the weathermen could make them, and their disaster-prone prose rose to new heights. The white cat watched from a safe window. It was her scene. I read my Christmas presents, *The English Poems of George Herbert* by Helen Wilcox, *Ravilious in Pictures, Sussex and the Downs* by James Russell, and the quite marvellous *At Large and At Small* by Anne Fadiman, 'the confessions of a literary hedonist'. It takes one to find one.

On the Sunday after Christmas, I rescued St Stephen from under seasonal trash. It is quite awful how the simple glories of the stall slide into murder and flight, and so quickly. And poor young Saul, guarding the coats. How do men live with the faces of those they killed? Although Paul said, 'I am what I am', and was not what he was, the wintry execution remained an icicle in his heart.

The earth was hard as iron, we sang, and the crib blocked my way to the pulpit. Today, the snow has gone, and the dead roses wave in the wind. Countless snowdrop tips prick through the mulch into the wood. It is very cold. Young friends come to lunch all the way from Dorset, leaving their baby behind. It might snow. You never know. Not these days.

Children of the Epiphany

POSSIBLY the frozen fields put me in mind of him, but I find myself immersed in Chekhov's short stories, a paperback that the bookseller found for me in his storeroom. He apologized that it should be such a flimsy edition. But it is perfect.

There is a painting of an onion-domed village church on the cover, below which two women chat in the snow. It is 1944, and millions were perishing on the Eastern Front. Should it happen to be the Epiphany, the Magi would have been forbidden entrance to the church. Outside, everything is waiting.

I read a story called 'Children', one of Chekhov's best, thought Tolstoy. It is marvellous. The grown-ups have gone out, and the servants are cutting out a dress in the kitchen. Four girls and a boy play an unnamed game for copecks. The girls are ladies; the boy is the cook's son. It is 1886. Yet it is now. It is the noise of any game, and it could be going on in any stuffy computerized bedroom at this moment, the unfairness, the absorption.

In the village, I hear of a friend's children tobogganing. Wormingford is hilly and slippery and immensely cold. It is

Twelfth Night, and dreadful lights will vanish from the gardens. In church, china kings and cows will be wrapped in tissue paper.

Someone has protested about the infantilizing of the Epiphany. It is full of children, of course, all those boys being carried up the Temple steps for registration, and soon to be murdered. John and the Christ-child. But it is not a childish feast. Never need one be more grown-up to comprehend it. It is all about recognition. It is about God and people finding themselves in the same situation. Was not life easier when they knew their place?

During the Epiphany, early on in this new light, St Paul advises us both to accept and to celebrate our differences. 'Be kindly affectioned one to another with brotherly love.' Few commands have been more ignored. He had walked and sailed all over the Roman world, and had seen how the empire had been able to absorb every kind of person, and some bizarre religions. Was there a moment when he thought that, if he set out the claims of this one in Rome itself, it would receive a similar tolerance?

Rome was an enlightened civilization. Greece had passed on its unquestionable light to it. But then comes this blinding light, with its blinding conviction of a higher authority than Caesar. No emperor was going to put up with that. And so the stamping out of this light began. But it was wildfire, luminous, travelling, flaring up there just when it had been put out here. Eventually, sovereigns in England would think it an honour to walk in the footsteps of the Magi who offered gold to a poor child who manifested God on earth.

Religious light is a form of darkness to some. 'Science gives off a clearer light,' they insist. Others see a dual illumination, the one interpreting the other. I see a steady light, and the brightest and best of the sons of the morning. It is light enough.

My parents told me that my first word was 'dark'. They were carrying an oil-lamp from room to room in the old house, and, as people do, one of them said, 'How dark it is!' And the other said, 'Yes, how dark it is! What a dark night!' And this several times. And the baby echoed, 'Dark'. This was not thought to be prophetic. Or, as they were waiting for 'Dad', ungrateful.

Owl Song

NOW and then, on Mondays and Fridays, I forget to collect the milk from its perch at Cockrell's Farm and walk up the track at near midnight. It is then that the valley owls cry. Byron said that only the rebuke 'I told you so' was sadder than owl songs.

But I don't find these sounds either melancholy or lonely. Tawny owls announce themselves with a shriek of 'ke-wick', then go operatic with a beautiful musical 'hoo-hoo-hoo', this followed with a long, tremulous 'oo-oo-oo-oo'.

I should add that I discovered this score in my birdsong book. It has been a birdsong end of the year with the centenary of Olivier Messiaen, a composer who was able to, well, compose from what he heard in the woods near Paris.

Religious mythology has libelled owls and most creatures, doing them great damage, but here, as 2008 closed, was a Christian mystic who went to the night opera and the dawn chorus for inspiration.

My Tawny owl roosts in the leggy hazels which arch over the deep gully and will now and then screech off in fury when the occasional car comes down. But on the midnight milk-run he will be silent-winged over the river singing his majestic solo, 'Hoo-hoo-hoo-oooooooo . . .' I will listen to him in bed, this time thinking, another year, another year.

The saint for New Year's Day is a monk named Almachius, who is said to have put a stop to the disgusting gladiatorial combats by running into the arena and separating the fighters, and getting killed himself, a brave action which so impressed the emperor Honorius that he put a stop to these cruel entertainments.

He comes to mind because, much to local joy, the Russian Orthodox Church has bought the Garrison Church at Colchester for £50,000. This is a fine wooden building from our Empire age, and far too good to be turned into some commercial enterprise. The icons are already set up, the rich liturgy already sounding.

A mile or two away they are excavating a Roman arena. The monk Almachius who ended death in the arena came from the East. Sea-birds from the nearby marshes, flying over, will note the sumptuous Orthodox singing, just as they would have looked down on endless church parades.

Set-aside having been banished, odd-shaped areas of fields have been left for the birds and other creatures. One of these runs alongside the fifty-acre field, from the crumbling bee bank to the badger sett.

I am re-reading my friend Richard Barber's English

translation of the Bodleian Library's *Bestiary or Book of Beasts*, which is the pre-Renaissance understanding of the animal kingdom, and which is about as far from David Attenborough as one can get. Real and fantasy creatures roam the world side by side, unicorns and mice.

What my owls would make of the *Bestiary*'s verdict on the 'Screech Owl' I dare not think: 'It is so called from its mourning and lamentation. When it cries it imitates either weeping or groaning . . . This bird signifies the wailing of sinners in hell.'

Barn owls are 'screech' owls, and rarer these days than Tawny owls. Pale and ghostly, Messiaen would have found it difficult to accommodate their wild shrieks in his bird music. But they are far from hellish, and are fond of people, making their home with farmers, who would hear them yapping and snoring in the rafters of their sheds, amiable birds actually.

It's Cold Outside

POTHOLES have appeared in the track, and along the lanes. I remember how shocked I was to bump over them in Manhattan. Snow and ice, and now rain, have achieved their sieve-like purpose.

Not to mention the last-minute descent of the oak leaves, which until yesterday blocked my winter river. Toiling in the half-light, banking the sludge, I freed the flow. Robins and wheatears helped. It was warm, almost sultry, and I liked to think that I could smell the spring. Not a soul about, the afternoon sky black and streaky gold, the silence meditative.

Then, hours at my desk. I am putting 30 years of John Clare essays into a book. The wonderful poet of the fields looks up at me, saying: 'Is this right? Are you sure?' The 30th essay has yet to be written. What more can I say? I may call the book 'At Helpston'. Titles are so committing. I have seen his birthplace only in summer, and have to take his word for what it looks like in January. Taking a writer's word is the least one can do.

A Helpston friend gave me his asylum photo for Christmas. It was taken by Mr Winter from Derby, in 1862, two years before his subject died. I see the photographer floating the plate in his darkroom, and the wary smile surfacing. Clare's eyes are youthful behind the cotton-wool brows, and his forehead rises like the Alps. He is challenging the lens to capture his likeness – holding back on it, as it were, as we sometimes do.

On Monday, we all went to St Mary the Virgin in Dedham to welcome the new Bishop of Chelmsford to our deanery. 'There is nothing at Dedham to hurt the eye' (Pevsner).

The Bishop's name is Stephen, and his being held up by a crash on the A12 allowed me to renew my acquaintance with memorials that shower the walls. His advice to us was to 'go forth' and not to hide away in our beautiful, and now comfortable, buildings. Take your purse and scrip, buy a sword, and then go forth.

Being the age many of us are, we have gone forth and returned home. Nevertheless, old evangels have their uses; so no excuses. This is the last message to the Dedham and Tey deanery before it is merged into Colchester. But

Dedham Church – what a marvel! The clothiers built it immediately before the Reformation – just got it done before the new direction. The grandeur of it! The forest of oaks, the seams of stone, the furlongs of glass in it. And, just ahead of me, a local grammar-school boy named John Constable. He certainly went forth.

People who garden long to do it in January. They know it is foolish, but the ache is there – to make a start. Plants themselves, once you get close to them, deny that there is nothing doing. Everything is doing. Rest itself is a kind of doing. It is something I assure my lazy self. And when I hear friends confess to their not rising until eight 'because it is still dark', I am shocked.

In one of Clare's poems, a father forces his teenage son out into the snow to feed the animals while he turns over, so to speak. The boy whistles, blows his fingers, calls. In Helpston, the young go forth with a song. What else can they do?

Jane Garrett

SPRING arrived today. The white cat and I, toasting our bottoms on opposing radiators, watched it through the window. For a few hours, January stepped down, and April stood up to be counted. How happy we were. As I collected the post, I marked a trickle of snowdrops in full bloom under the Garrya tassels, and heard a new warmth in the birdsong. I felt no increase in the sun's warmth. But it shone for all it was worth.

More wily charity pleas among the letters. They reminded me of the old friend whose only post they were. She wrote a little cheque to each and every one of them, flattered that they should have thought of her, some of them with a message to her from the Prince of Wales, or the Mayor of Colchester. She could afford it, we knew, eating like a fly, as she did, making my coffee after church with 20 grains of instant: 'You must tell me if it's too strong.' Dear, good, always-missed Helen.

The spring reminds me of one of those singers who announce a gala appearance for two days only, as did Joan Sutherland when I was in New York, gloriously waking up the city, and changing everything, if only for a couple of hours.

Fay Weldon on the radio, silvery voiced, provocative. She reads Jane Austen's unfinished novel, *Sanditon*, wickedly. Which makes me search for my copy and continue as far as it goes. It sends up the seaside as a cure-all.

I meet my new GP, and wait for her in the little room among the old chaps. Although I am as old or even older than they are, I opt out of their years, this being the only way to be young at my age. A new doctor is a new landmark in one's life, the old one having retired at the indulgent age of 65. Would Fay Weldon or I do a thing like that? Would we not type 'Chapter One' on a new page? Although Shakespeare did not. He wrote 'Finis', and then went back to Stratford to be a gentleman.

We sang Percy Dearmer's 'Unto us a boy is born' at the Little Horkesley patronal festival, and I thought of my old, very dear, now long-dead friend, Jane. Dearmer had married her parents. They had 'anticipated' their marriage, thus having to leave Suffolk for Norfolk, where nothing would be known. All this in 1915, and they artists and the like. Unto them a girl was born. She married a Cambridge botanist. And so it went on, irregularly but lovingly. Not to say brilliantly.

Jane had a way of losing her place in the hymn book, and sometimes someone near her would take it from her hand and find it. Her uncle composed 'Hills of the North, rejoice'. Maybe she sings it in heaven in her cracked mezzo-soprano. What a mercy it is that when our best friends go they leave their best earthly parts with us. Such generosity. And Paul's lovely hedge-laying, of course.

I went to the stationers and laid-in A4 and carbons and the like, enough for a siege, and I thought of Shakespeare dumping his quills and parchment. No more *Much Ado About Nothing*. Just respectability, and one's arms over the fireplace. And the spring sometimes looking through the window in January. And a not-too-demanding Lent.

On Pendle Hill

A STRANGE day. Two hours of brilliant sunshine, and many hours of freezing fog. Except it isn't freezing – just as cold, but liquid, lanes all sloppy mud, and the wetness being blown out of the trees by a slight wind.

I would have stayed indoors, but for urgent business with our village post office – for which God be praised. Heather emerges from what Thomas Hardy called 'her penetralia' to sell me three books of stamps, and I find myself remembering a lifetime of country shopkeepers who briefly emerged from a curtained holy-of-holies to serve me; and that never once have I seen inside these secret rooms. But then their potent mystery would be gone for ever. Heather and I tell each other what a ghastly day it is. And then she's gone.

Back at the farmhouse, Jonathan has taken my rubbish up to the top for the dustmen. It sways garishly on his muddy runabout, a basic little vehicle, which looks as if it is constructed out of Meccano. The dustmen are exacting, and have to be waited on hand and foot according to the conservation faith. It is a blue day: bottles, Whiskas tins, and the *Times*.

Ten thousand starlings fly over, all talking at once. And then comes the wondrous sight that I could not have seen yesterday, and can only just make out today, as the light is so bad: scores of matt-white snowdrop heads in the mulch below the quince tree.

The white cat sits on a brick surveying them, or rather surveying why I am hanging about in weather like this when it is tea-time.

The Epiphany weeks pass. We are to remember George Fox. I went to find him once on Pendle Hill, in Lancashire. He had been travelling about for a decade before, aged 28, he saw Pendle Hill rising out of Bowland, like, William Penn said, 'a great auditory'. What a natural pulpit it would have made.

But, descending, Fox mounted a haystack and said nothing, not a word, to his expectant congregation of Seekers. This was the first Quaker sermon – silence. He had a young friend with him, Richard Farnsworth, who had been hurt in some way and so was unable to climb Pendle: how regularly people have climbed mountains to find God.

I must admit that when I climbed Pendle in the rain, I was as keen to take in that mighty view as that inner voice that would create the Society of Friends. Also, I had been reading David Pownall's wonderful book *Between Ribble and Lune*, and was still caught up in his vision of Lancashire. And I, too, had left a companion at the bottom, my dear hospitable friend Allen, nice and dry in the car.

Thomas Carlyle wrote that perhaps the most remarkable incident in modern history is not the Diet of Worms, still less the Battle of Waterloo, but George Fox making himself a suit of Leather! And he quoted the quiet craftsman's words: 'Will all the shoe-wages under the Moon ferry me across into that far Land of Light? Only Meditation can, and devout Prayer to God. I will to the woods: the hollow of a tree will lodge me, wild berries feed me; and for Clothes, cannot I stitch myself one perennial suit of Leather?' Thus, continues Carlyle, 'from the lowest depth there is a path to the loftiest height'.

I suppose he meant from cobbling to Pendle Hill; from being a tradesman to being a prophet.

Words in Sand

LIKE everyone else – I trust – in the Church of England, I have been reading and watching Diarmaid MacCulloch's *A*

History of Christianity. It has been sweeping me along, racing me through the centuries, confirming my prejudices, challenging my dullness, waking me up.

And none more so than when it deals with Time. How recent this faith is. Half as old as the pyramids, and a fraction as old as some of the bones that Sir David Attenborough handles. What a new teaching! I can say this as someone who lives a mile from a Neolithic settlement, and six miles from a Roman city.

Those who lived in the settlement were sharpening our local flints 3000 years before Christ was born, and those who built the city did so while he was being born. And yet his Church has had a way of presenting itself as older than the hills. It is in fact a very modern structure, as this Suffolk clergyman's son reminds us. And, recognizing this, it makes the Christian recognize himself or herself as a novel being, not some remnant of an antiquated religion – which is not a bad thought for New Year's Day.

A book I would read in tandem with Professor MacCulloch is *The Sayings of Jesus*, selected by Andrew Linzey. Here are all the words that he said, and here is the stupendous structure that we made of them. And let them be a lesson to us in 2010. The brief gospel, the never-ending commentary called the Church. The only words that Jesus wrote were by his finger, in sand, whereas his followers write about his teachings and stories and poems incessantly. As for his illiterate leaders, look what they made of what he said. But it is 1 January, and we must be Christian, and look for the best in the world.

Those of us who keep diaries will be keeping them with a vengeance at this moment. January is the most diarized month. Wait until April, and see the entries petering out. Though not for the diarist proper.

'I wonder why I do it?' wrote Virginia Woolf, who, every teatime, allowed her pen to run wild over the events of the day.

James Boswell thought: 'I should live no more than I can record.' And the Revd James Hervey told himself: 'Compile a secret history of your heart and conduct.'

But, as we know, usually to our delight, most diaries are apt to be the histories of other people's hearts and conducts. Great diaries are usually great literature. Francis Kilvert, the curate of Clyro, did not dash his down like Virginia Woolf, but worked on it as she did her novels and was human enough to half-hope that, deeply private as it was, someone would read it and know 'that I existed'.

Now and then I read from Kilvert's hauntingly wonderful diary in church. This really would have amazed him. Robert Fothergill has called the diary 'the book of the self'. Stefan Kanfer said that a diary starts out as a kind of looking-glass that reflects the diarist, and ends up by reflecting the reader.

Diaries are legion. They create a direct entrée to a vanished society and to another moment. Gossip pours through them, but so does revelation of the highest kind. Samuel Pepys wrote his masterpiece diary in a beautiful shorthand, and it floods the Restoration years with a brilliance that can never be surpassed.

Huge numbers of diaries are in print, and huge numbers of them lie unpublished in attics and local archives. Few are unreadable – at least for 'January'.

Absent Relations

THE QUESTION most asked if you live in a funny old house in the middle of nowhere is: 'Do you see ghosts?' No; but now and then I hear mothers calling 'Get up!' They stand at the bottom of the clumsy stairs, or the wonky ladder to the attic, threatening sleepy sons with dire consequences if they do not appear before they count ten. Feed the pigs. Go to school. What would their father say? Half-past five and still abed.

But at least these centuries of farmers' boys would not likely have put their parents down on paper. Many writers do, one way or another. Dickens immortalized – and forgave – his father in Mr Micawber. Edmund Gosse, an only son, in his masterpiece, *Father and Son*, revealed how far one could go in not giving hurt to a parent. Poor Mr Gosse Snr was a Creationist, and also a great scientist. Genesis told him one thing, the rocks, another. He and his fellow religionists once stood on the shore to await the Second Coming. One day Edmund told him that he did not believe a word of all this. Love continued between them, but something terrible, as well. It was not the usual row – literature saw to that. But what a fate, to breed an author!

The poet John Clare had to break it to his parents gently that he had written what he read to them because his mother 'knew not a single letter, and superstition went so far with her that she believed the higher parts of learning was the blackest arts of witchcraft'. Oh, the shame of it, to have a writer for a son! Or a daughter, of course. And, oh, the risk of it!

My friend Edward Blishen was able to take the risk. Love

16

made it possible for him. 'Hate could be equally rewarding.' The plain truth was that his mother, Lizzie Pye, a servant girl and all unknowingly a great woman, was irresistible copy.

On the whole, writers find fathers easier to expose than they do mothers; not that exposure is necessarily a driving force – only the morality of telling the truth. To tell the truth about Mother, one had to cut into oneself as well as into her.

Edward and Lizzie seem to have been unflinching in this all their lives, which is not usually the case. But she had to grow old before he could, at least, show her to others as unsparingly as, since his boyhood, she had shown herself to him. For such a passionate writer, it was a long wait. Both he and his mother were touchers to the end – embracing, holding hands, giving little kisses: a warming existence. And this helped.

Iciness can be equally productive. Think of Ivy Compton-Burnett's *Mother and Son*. Yet there is a kind of natural avoidance, to the extent of caricature, in putting parents on the page. Once, Jesus shockingly rebuffed his mother – 'Woman, what have I to do with you?' The clinging nature of Jewish mothers?

With writers, of course, there is the painful nature of all ties, and their exploration, the putting them into words, and the breaking of taboos, the flight from them, and the inescapable tentacles of them, which the playwright Dodie Smith called *Dear Octopus*. Thus, from afar, in rooms where parents and children have insisted on dependence and independence for many generations, I might catch a cry or two. Although, of course, it might be the white cat.

FEBRUARY

Reverend Women

MATINS with morning tea. Very early. The sun tips the fields with indescribable glory. Thousands of starlings wing north on a bird Haj. Am I approaching Lent, or is Lent approaching me?

It is dreadfully cold, and the Bemerton servants will be making the fires up for Mr Herbert, who is unwell. Is he at prayer, or at his lute? It will be the same thing. This time last year I was sleeping in his rectory. Vikram, Judy, and I were being taught to sing a hymn, 'The Flower':

Who would have thought my shrivel'd heart
Could have recover'd greennesse? It was gone
Quite under ground; as flowers depart
To see their mother-root, when they have blown;
Where they together
All the hard weather,
Dead to the world, keep house unknown.

I visit my woodland snowdrops. They are as multitudinous as the starlings, but so still. And tall. I have never been able to keep pace with their variety, and I view them as teachers view their classes of multiracial children, finding them, each kind, lovely. The Van Gogh sun goes in, and it starts to snow thinly. Sunday will be Quinquagesima, when they will bury George Herbert, dead to the world, the Epistle for which is St Paul's peroration on Love, in which he first peers through a glass darkly, then sees Love 'face to face'.

The row over women bishops reminds me of an incident in Sylvia Townsend Warner's novel *The Corner that Held Them*, when three medieval women who have founded a damp priory in the Fens, and who are holy and educated, irritably await the arrival of an ignorant and not very holy man to bring them the Sacrament. I knew Sylvia Townsend Warner, and all I can say is that the General Synod should thank heaven that she isn't a member. She always reminded me of Hilda of Whitby, who, you will recall, was the abbess of a male and female community.

St Paul's beautiful words on love made me think again of the women in his ministry, and how he left so many things to them. Women such as Priscilla, the wife of Aquila, 'and the church that is in their house'; Phoebe, 'servant to the church'; Mary, 'the mother of John Mark'; Dorcas the dressmaker; Rhoda, who opened the door with gladness to Peter; Tryphena and Tryphosa, 'who labour in the Lord'; and particularly Lydia, the seller of purple cloth, who held prayer meetings by the river, a favourite of mine.

But St Paul can – to us – be contradictory, expressing in the strongest terms his approval of the conventional attitudes of his day towards the sexes, and yet writing things such as 'There is neither male nor female, for you are all one in Christ Jesus.' He says: 'I suffer not a woman to teach . . . but to be in silence,' and then, 'Have we not power to lead about a sister, a wife, as well as other apostles?' The Lord himself was of course shockingly indifferent to sexuality. Who were nearest to him at the appalling end? Who at the birth of his Church? Bishop – Greek *episkopos* – *skopos* – watcher. 'While shepherds watched their flocks by night.' Shepherdesses . . .

Sudbury, Suffolk

WATER, water everywhere. Especially in Water Lane. Particularly in black lakes that gather in front of modern houses where some old field ditch has been blocked with asphalt. The traffic raises it in curtains.

I trespass on my neighbour's lawn in order to get through to the village, not wearing my wellingtons. Nayland, where I shop, reminds me that its name means 'an island'. But the Stour keeps its banks, and there are few of the grim lakes in the hollows of the corn. The farmhouse is so artfully set as to dodge the water-table of the river, standing dry and aloof. Oceans have poured past it. The stones in the track have been washed like gold dust. Several thousand snowdrops are out.

This morning it is warm; last evening it was bitter. John has kindly climbed a tall ladder to drag his hand along the guttering to tip little dams of old nest twigs and moss, the residue of last year's birds' building site down to the flower-bed, and now I can lie in bed and listen to gallons of rainwater gurgling along a foot from my head.

I am to have a road named after me in my native town, Sudbury, in Suffolk. Strictly speaking, I was born three miles from it in a village called Acton. So is Mark Catesby, the naturalist. Where will they be, these roads? Not in the water-meadows, for sure. These are where we played.

Sudbury is a Y-shaped Saxon borough that fell into disrepute as a Rotten Borough. The wicked young journalist Charles Dickens renamed it Eatanswill in *Pickwick Papers*. But this was long before my time, and long after Mark Catesby's time.

He was an artist-botanist, who went to the Carolinas and wrote and illustrated two glorious books in the early eighteenth century, *The Natural History of Carolina, Florida and the Bahama Islands, with Observations on the Soil, Air and Water*. And then, a few years later, came another wonderful work, *Hortus Britanno-Americannus, or a Collection of 85 Curious Trees and Shrubs, the Production of North America, Adapted to the Climate and Soil of Great Britain*. These beautiful volumes contain some 150 of Catesby's marvellous flower paintings.

Our names will be where no one lived when we were boys, in pastures, on farmland, on hopeful estates. But it is a strange thing at this moment, not for the great Catesby, but for me, to have residents giving my name as their address – rather like seeing Timbuktu on the Norwich line.

The churches are steadying themselves for Lent. I like the interim Sundays. In the old country days, February was ploughing time, shepherding time. John Clare writes of wet streets, warm walls, cautious emergence from winter rooms and barns, though still 'Frost breathes upon the stiff'ning stream, And numbs it into ice'. So watch out.

We are to read Mark and Timothy, youthful writers. St Mark goes along at a fine pace; Timothy's Letters are from St Paul. Timothy is the son of a mixed marriage between a

Jew and a pagan. He is Paul's envoy to Ephesus, Thessaly, and Corinth, and 'my own son in the faith'. He is 'my son Timothy'. He is Bishop Timothy, though no one is to despise his youth. 'O Timothy, keep that which is committed to thy trust.' How the love of the old man for his pupil travels through time.

Wild Places

THEY told me that the hunt would be coming through, but I had forgotten. All nature changes when the hunt comes through. Coming down from the study, I find the white cat shivering behind the ancient clock and thinking – the hunt! But you have a strong door and a moderately sized man to protect you, I tell her. This is no comfort, apparently; for she shakes the more. It is the hound 'music', wild and wicked. Exultant. It howls over the hill.

Now, when David the naturalist's collie bursts in on Saturday, yelling his head off, whacking the furniture with his tail, the cat doesn't shift. Simply looks down on him. Purrs, even. Thus the huntsman's hounds sound a very different note – that of terror. Creatures quake in setts, burrows, and nests, and the animal kingdom is frightened.

Terror is hard to communicate in literature. The more the terror writers try, the more unterrifying they are. Ronan Bennett's novel *Havoc in its Third Year* is a masterpiece about this emotion. Everything is understated – 'normal'. It is about a recusant Catholic family being hounded by keen Protestants in the seventeenth century. A quotation from

Goethe prefaces it: 'Mistrust all in whom the desire to punish is imperative.' One remembers Saul/Paul. But the genius of the story lies in its terror.

The white cat stopped shaking eventually, as did all the creatures of the valley. The hound music died away. I thought of Christ's natural terror in Gethsemane. And of the Jews hearing the Nazis singing, their locked doors no safety, and their knowing this.

Lent once more. What shall my discipline be? Rather than fast I will say Compline before I sleep. Also feed on George Herbert. And recognize that the wilderness is not the wasteland. Naturalist friends have made this plain. Our East Anglian wilderness spread across the Norfolk-Suffolk border and was called the Breckland, but the Forestry Commission destroyed it a century ago. We still miss it. It is where they filmed *Dad's Army*. Prehistoric people dwelt there, as they did on most of our moors, preferring its openness.

I felt their presence when I walked on Rannoch Moor, Bodmin Moor, and many a wild place. Sometimes I saw their hearths. And I certainly saw their views, wide, unclouded, sometimes seaward. They liked an open life. The religious imagery of the desert conflicts with nature's realities. But then we come to Christ's privations and the prospect before him, and all is another matter.

The poet George Crabbe understood the botany of the Aldeburgh marshes, and found an intellectual and spiritual fulfilment in them. But he banished Peter Grimes there, a man who did not understand his own wickedness. Or could not. That was his tragedy.

Writers have been partial to deserts: Shakespeare with

his blasted heath, Hardy with his Egdon Heath, now mostly ploughed up. But in *The Return of the Native* he allowed its furze to destroy all the best of the community that had settled there. Love, literature, beauty – all was gnawed away by grit, prickly plants, and lizards. Long ago, the inhabitants of the Essex marshes and of the Fens were thought barely human. 'Then was Jesus led up of the Spirit into the wilderness.'

With George Herbert

TO BEMERTON, to take part in the BBC Sunday-morning service from George Herbert's church. Salisbury is pencil-grey and cold running to raw. Yet spring-like. I have put down roots there over the years, and there is a faint sense of coming home. The Cathedral spire is a faint smudge against the colourless sky.

Canon Judy Rees meets me on the otherwise empty platform, and at once there is huge happiness. We walk to the tiny church, which is busy with technicians, the Farrant Singers, composers, conductors, musicians, and, of course, George Herbert. In fact, so 'filling' and fulfilling is the poet that there is not really any space for the rest of us.

But here we are, knowing our place, preparing to worship in an Anglican shrine. We are to go out 'live', although our rehearsals are far from dead. It is the constant marvel of Herbert that he cannot die. How young and fresh he is, how well. And he so sick when he crept across the lane to sing the office, his fingers on this same door-handle.

Before we begin, I cross to the Rectory to describe his bedchamber, a tall version of my own with wide floorboards and a stone casement opening on the Nadder. The river is high and glittering, the sloping lawn smooth for February. An ancient man has mown it. Everything to do with the BBC service has had to be scripted; so we measure words, chopping out a paragraph, counting a sentence.

It was in this room that Herbert handed a fat bundle of manuscripts to Mr Ferrar's man from Little Gidding with the instruction, 'Tell your master, if they are any good, please publish these poems. If not, burn them.' On Quinquagesima Sunday 1633, he was buried a few steps from his bed. It was a strange year. King Charles went to Little Gidding, William Laud went to Canterbury, John Donne published his poems, too.

This Saturday night, I slept in the room adjoining Herbert's, meaning to read for an hour or so, but was so close to him that all I could do was to stare into the great empty fireplace opposite and imagine its heat.

A few hours later, Vikram Seth and I had morning tea by the Aga, and hastened across the road for the live performance, the enchanting words, the new music, the old language, the young priest-poet's enduring love and wit, the 46th Rector of Bemerton, Simon, in his seat, and for me the sound of a lute and what I am sure would have been a true voice, though in what key who can tell?

Having once edited Herbert's *A Priest to the Temple*, his fearfully strict Rule for parsons, I did my best to describe the rural church in his day in the BBC's brief allowance of words. But the achievement of the service seemed to have little to do with us, and everything to do with the Herbertian love that 'bade us welcome', and that flooded the building. Bemerton means 'the home of the trumpeters'. In 'Church-Musick', Herbert writes: 'Sweetest of Sweets, I thank you.'

At choral evensong in Salisbury Cathedral that afternoon, Vikram, Alison, Judy and I, and Stephen, the BBC's perfectionist creator of the George Herbert service, listened to another, later music, that of Herbert Howells, as we sat where he joined in every Thursday, crossing the water-meadows to taste this holy sound. Because it 'knows the way to heaven's door'.

Plough Sunday

A RESIDUAL devotion to, usually, some abandoned rite hangs around in the village memory. Little that takes place in the fields these days rings a bell in church. Barry the ringer told me how he found himself in the real world at a Plough Sunday service in Bures.

Bures bridges itself across both Suffolk and Essex, and is where, traditionally, the 15-year-old Edmund was crowned King of East Anglia. The Stour has been thinly flooded across its water-meadows since Christmas and glinting with birds.

Plough Sunday – it should have been Monday – comes after Twelfth Night. Barry and I are old enough to find it normal enough – only, as such things happen, progress, being the tractor, displaced it. And this now long ago.

When I first came to live here, my neighbour William Brown, who farmed above me, asked me how to take Plough Sunday service. He was a Scot from Ayrshire, whose father had emigrated from that stony ground to our rich but half-lost soil. So we found a hand-plough among the iron litter, tied yellow ribbons to its handles, and stood it on the chancel step of Little Horkesley church.

A plough had for everlasting represented the very essence of agriculture. When a rural congregation saw it just below the altar, there was barely a need for office or sermon; while the hymn itself sprang from the share. It would have been painted blue. Ploughmen – called horsemen in our sliver of the world – made themselves obvious. And thus it had been for ever and ever, amen.

When it went, nobody brought a tractor into church. I can't recall what I said or what we sung, but the beautiful plough from the dead bindweed held our gaze.

Ploughmen, horsemen, walked hippity-hop, one foot in the furrow, one foot on its crest. Up and down, up and down, all winter's day, turning at the top, thinking of – what? Now there's a question.

W. B. Yeats wrote:

All things uncomely and broken, all things worn out
    and old,
The cry of a child by the roadway, the creek of a
    lumbering cart,
The heavy steps of the plowman, splashing the wintry
    mold,
Are wronging your image that blossoms a rose in the
    deeps of my heart.

The once most commonplace of country sights and sounds are eroding the poets' finer thoughts. John Clare preferred ploughing to gardening. Solitary in a vast field, there was no one to see that he was composing, no one to witness 'my muttering'. He made lines across Helpston's acres and, later on by the cottage fire, lines across paper, working double time. I possess a few ears of corn from a field where he ploughed, crisp, precious, though tractor-sown.

I have been shifting leaves by the million. Damp and dry, they leave new grass and yellowing grass, which will turn green. All in good time. My wood is delicately spiky with unopened snowdrops. It is hard to be inside. They are manuring up at the top, and the commuters' smart cars are spraying the muck, which is thoughtful of them.

The Word and The Worm

THE SHROVE Tuesday sun spun up between the ash tree and Duncan's generator, as bright as a button. It gilded my tea mug, and glorified the white cat who, as usual, was glaring through the window at the blackbirds.

The window contains an ancient IHS stained-glass medallion that Ian found in Framlingham. It is fixed to the pane with Uno glue. The morning sun, being as bright as it can be, burns through it. Henry, the Vicar, will be walking to our minute school – 13 pupils – to toss pancakes.

There are two figures on the hilltop: a girl leading a horse, and a young man descending from it with light steps, his face ablaze. He carries something under his arm which, when he opens it, is also golden and blinding. He tells us that it is something called the Word. He holds it above his head. He has yellow hair, and he came from the north. The Word glitters like sunshine.

In the afternoon, I rake up oak leaves, prior to the first mow. It is bitterly cold and wonderfully hot at the same time. The new grass is springy, and Wordsworth's wild daffodils make a fine patch in the orchard. Kate is walking her new puppy, a chocolate-coloured animal of unrestrained joy. She is training her, she says. An old joke comes into my head: 'I am a dog. My name is Sit.'

I pick a few primroses for the table. I think of Ash Wednesday and of Joel. 'Let the priest, the ministers of the Lord, weep between the porch and the altar.' Henry won't be weeping. He will be burning last year's palms to make ash for our foreheads. I re-read T. S. Eliot's 'Ash Wednesday 1930'.

If the lost word is lost, if the spent word is spent
If the unheard, unspoken
Word is unspoken, unheard;
Still is the unspoken word, the Word unheard,
The Word without a word, the Word within
The world and for the world;
And the light shone in darkness and
Against the Word the unstilled world still whirled
About the centre of the silent Word.

The fair young man with the Book walks through the land and opens its illuminated pages, calling out: 'Don't forget, you first heard it here!' Heaven knows what most of us made of it – this 'Word'.

Pip brings me our parish magazine, a monthly called *The Worm*, whose masthead is a dragon having a virgin for supper. Her white legs dangle from its jaws. But St George comes riding in; so maybe all is not lost.

Considering the inactivity of the village when I walk through it, its recorded activity is alarming. Somebody is going to line the bus shelter, free of charge. Should we keep the telephone box? The village-hall sign still has not arrived – 'The Recreation Trust has been asking for this for a very long time.'

Christopher writes about the Wormingford-to-Abberton pipeline and its funding. 'Eight years on, and we are still waiting.' Andrew, our archaeologist, tells us about Giles Barnardiston, the Quaker, who lived on our height above the Stour with his wife, Philippa, and who found the Word in quietness.

Bill and his dog, Cyrus, see a pair of otters in the river. As a boy, I witnessed an otter hunt – a disgusting business.

Spectacles

I AM at the optician's. We sit in a shop window, in various degrees of darkness and light. We are being framed at vast expense, or, in my case, being updated. We go to tiny rooms, and read the chart. The optician, who is about 25, won't have to do this for donkey's years. He has lustrous eyes, like a Gainsborough portrait.

The black discs drop in and out; the giant letters dwindle to nothingness. 'What do you see?' What a question. He cleans my old specs, to my shame. 'Your sight hasn't changed much.'

About four feet below us runs the road along which the Emperor Claudius was driven to his temple, where he would be made a god. But I am in the optician's chair, not the barber's chair, and I must not distract his attention with this kind of local information. So I sit, stock-still, as the letters diminish, tumble about, tell him things about me which I will never know.

I think of the Revd Patrick Brontë having his cataracts removed with a knife. Charlotte held his hand. The bandages were removed after a month's blindfold, and, glory to God, he could see. She began to write *Jane Eyre* in the lodgings, while all the time there lurked the terrible possibility of sightlessness for the rest of his days. The Manchester life clattered below. I wait for the bill. My expert sight-giver says, 'Next.'

The old high street is drab. The cuts are having their effect. Sale, sale, sale – but no customers. The bravura town hall is white in the afternoon sun. St Helena, clasping the True Cross, stands on top of it. She was Romano-British and the mother of Constantine. Is she the patron saint of archaeologists?

She would remember morning coffee in the restaurants below, the dressed shop windows, the departed elegance, the public library service – marvellous, this – and the gentlemen-only bar at the Red Lion, where a Manet-like lady kept a roaring fire. All gone, all gone.

Should the cuts come within a stone's throw of our

public libraries, let us all cry out. Increasingly, the Government seems to have its eye so firmly fixed on the red that it can no longer see the wealth on the opposite page. The young never-employed – through no fault of their own – laugh in doorways. The regiment from the barracks is in Afghanistan.

I write in the mornings; that is, when I am not in one or other of my market towns, seeing economic sights and visiting their fine public libraries; and I pull the garden round after lunch, so that the bulbs won't be put to shame in a week or two.

Frost has broached one of the springs that everlastingly bubble beneath the Big Field, and a sparkling new stream finds its way to the Stour. Alas, this cannot go on. My head turns to hardcore, to fill-in, or whatever. This year and wherever, water thinks that it can do what it likes.

How the robins sing! How the catkins shake! How once more that vengeful man on the Damascus road hoves into view with his list of victims. And that 'Why are you doing this?' – a question we all might ask ourselves. And then that blinding stab of the Epiphany light, and the subsequent helplessness. Then the turnaround.

I de-mulch the snowdrops.

Voices

TWO books have joined each other on the library table, and will most likely stay there for many a long year. One is Andrew Linzey's extraction from the *Gospels of The Sayings of Jesus*, the other is Diarmaid MacCulloch's vast *A History of Christianity*. The Lord's few words and the Church's non-stop interpretation of them. The wonderful still small voice, and the cosmic row. Here, side by side, is Christ and Christianity. They leave the reader to conclude where or if they differ.

Professor Linzey writes: 'The sayings of Jesus have changed our world, inspiring countless poets, painters, and musicians, as well as saints and theologians. They have brought hope to the dying, and solace to the wretched. To millions, they are a source of divine inspiration. 'As the first Christians broke bread and shared the cup, they brought into remembrance the words of Jesus which gave them life and hope. This collection of his most famous sayings . . . gives a picture of the man whom many revere as the Son of God and whose life has had an incalculable influence on Western history and culture.'

Professor MacCulloch writes: 'Religious belief can be very close to madness. It has brought human beings to acts of criminal folly as well as to the highest achievements of goodness, creativity, and generosity. I tell the story of both extremes.'

At matins in the village church, tender expressions of the faith over the Christian centuries tumble across each other. Plus the words which Jesus repeated in the synagogue or in the open air. David's poem, 'Yet have I set my King upon my holy hill of Sion'; the *Te Deum Laudamus* – almost certainly not by St Ambrose and St Augustine, but so perfect; Job's natural history read in Brian's strong voice; Joseph Addison's thankfulness for being alive; George Matheson's emotional tracing the rainbow through the rain; Cranmer's blessing; all this said in an hour by 16 voices. And as best we could.

And the faith so youthful, with Roman nails lying on the kitchen table. So how did His words, that simple rural stream of talk, wisdom, and renewed law – and entertaining tales – for example become the Vatican Library? Or my bookshelf bursting at the seams?

Anyway, another David has arrived, one who reads 'Book at Bedtime' to us, or novels on audio, and who goes to church and to his allotment in the middle of London. And who, thankfully, has brought a chain-saw with him, for February is for coppicing and tidying the wood. The chain-saw sings in the hazels. The logs are neatly piled in the dry for next winter. Last February's firewood spits in the stove.

In the morning, very early, the old house feels different – feels very cold, to be accurate. A blob has got into the oil pipe, presumably. And I hear the warming-up sounds of childhood in my imagination, the clink of kindling on the hearth, the raking of cinders, the silent acceptance of this chill in the rooms which, when nothing could be done about it, was not unenjoyable. Although the white cat is less philosophical, and is saying: 'Why keep these men if they can't keep one warm?'

But I know how to poke a boiler into life. There is a roar and a promise.

Jeremiah's Book

MID-LENT, and Jeremiah, a stunning writer. He is the master of reproach. There is a legend that they stoned him to death; for a nation cannot stand reproach. A modern writer calls him the most personal and sensitive of the Old Testament prophets, and he certainly gets under the skin.

Not that he wanted his role, backing away from it and telling God, 'I cannot speak; for I am a child.' God was not having any of this. 'Say not, "I am a child",' and he touched Jeremiah's mouth. Thus the divine language I am reading this cold Lent day. He lived 700 years before Christ, who would often have read him. As did the Jews in the concentration camps.

God said to Jeremiah: 'What do you see?' He saw an almond branch, bitter, bitter. His book is about returning, coming back. Shockingly, the pastors themselves have destroyed the sacred, the holy vineyard. Pashur, who was governor of the temple, wasn't having this, and he put Jeremiah in the stocks. God's reply to this was 'to make Pashur a terror to himself'. What more dreadful fate?

Looking at the photos in the financial press, I see what God means. People helplessly entangled in money and frightened stiff. Today's Jacob Marleys.

Because no one listened to his spoken warnings, Jeremiah got his friend Baruch to write them down and give his book to the King. It was winter, and the King was sitting by the fire. As he read the Book of Jeremiah, he cut the page off with his penknife and burnt it. The Nazis made bonfires of wise books.

On and on I read, and into Jeremiah's lamentations – 'How is the gold become dim!' How indeed.

I suppose that I could think figuratively about the brambles that have grown at length in my hedge and among the roses, but, of course, I know perfectly well why they are there. It is because last year I only cut them off and did not dig them up. When my friends bought the old farmhouse in 1943, they had to more or less machete their way through the blackberries to the front door, they said.

A million snowdrops are losing their whiteness. A pair of magpies are boasting theirs. Big, nervous birds, they do everything in couples, bouncing down to feed – then away! The white cat makes outraged noises on the other side of the kitchen window. Why do birds exist? she asks God. Bouncing around, flying about, singing up high. Disturbing the peace. Two legs.

A village funeral. Somebody's wedding flowers, still lovely. Somebody's field for all the cars. The little coffin of the old familiar friend who was walking into his 90s, and who played the organ on occasion, and always a particular hymn and a particular chant. He had a cathedral-size voice.

Barry kindly picks me up and takes me to the church. It is full to the brim, mostly with sensible-looking men in good overcoats. His daughter tells us about his life, which, of course, we all knew. The secret is to make the familiar service sound fresh, sound thrilling, even. And this Henry, our priest, does well.

In the chancel, I am left with the famously impossible-to-sit-on chair, a piece of furniture not unlike a heraldic commode. This because the choir is in full strength. Thoughts run into each other: death, paradise, tea.

MARCH

On the Saxon Shore

TWO young Mancunian executioners arrive at the door, sweetly smiling, as executioners do. They wave the warrant in my face. See, my signature. The oak stump must die. For too long it has put out tentative approaches to the farm generator, causing a nervous frisson through the neighbourhood.

The executioners quell its suspicions by appearing in a pretty little van called Contract Arborists, and not an axe in sight. The oak stump is about 12 feet high and 50 years old. A *Reine Victoria* rose clings to it in summer. But this is winter; Lent, even. So a sad whine fills the valley as the woodmen do their duty. All morning they work, coppicing hazel, banking sawdust, now and then going off on scampers in the dank meadow like puppies. The generator looks sparky.

I preach on St Cedd at evensong, sensing that this is what he might like. Not that it is his day, but it is nice to be talked about when it isn't one's day. Lindisfarne was a Celtic university, art college, and theological training centre, which trained 12 Saxon boys to become missionaries to their own people, who distrusted Celts, finding them too happy. Life had to be grim if Valhalla was to be a treat.

When he grew up, they sent him to the East Saxons, who

lived in an oak wood, worshipping trees and weather. Carrying a beautiful painted book above his yellow head, Cedd talked of love. Not liking forests, he found a ready-made church on the Saxon shore named Othona, where he could sing along with the tides and sea birds. Two of his tree churches remain, Polstead and Yeldham, and we biked to look at them when we were children.

There is an Anglo-Saxon poem, 'The Husband's Message', which might almost be describing Cedd's mission to Essex.

Now that we're alone I can explain
The secret meaning of this stage.
I was once a child,
But now one of the sons of men, living far from here,
Sends me on errands over the salt streams,
Commends me to carry a cunningly carved letter.
At my master's command I have often crossed the sea,
Sailed in the ship's hold to strange destinations.
And this time I have come especially
To show assurance in your mind
About my lord's great love for you.

Kevin Crossley-Holland translated this, and it has an open quality, which allows an immense idea to enter.

As I preached – if one can call it preaching – it poured, the rain splashing on the church roof, just as it rained when I walked to Lindisfarne, torrentially, the Northumbrian sea stabbed and pricked with water-javelins, my body, too. And the Celtic Jesus remained soaked in the rocks. But when I read poems at Othona, that barn of a shrine howled drily in the east wind.

Cedd's pulpit oak at Yeldham is corseted in iron stays, and quite dead. But his pulpit oak at Polstead has been born again.

Memory Bank

SURPRISINGLY, 'memory' makes but half-a-dozen appearances in the King James Bible, although 'remembrance' and 'remember' are everywhere. The psalmist, in one of his wild torrents of rage, turns on his detractors: let God 'cut off the memory of them from the earth'. Later, he will assure his Lord that future generations 'shall abundantly utter the memory of thy great goodness'.

There are two references that, in all probability, there will be no memory of when we are dead; and there is St Paul's schoolmasterly instruction to his pupils at Corinth that they should 'keep in memory what I preached unto you', the gospel of Christ, no less.

'What a good memory you have!' they tell me in church. They are referring to the writer's baggage-train of colourful oddments and scatterings of scholarship, plus his bookish knack to find the place. I have to refrain from burdening them with some of the things I have committed to memory, such as the whole of *The Rubáiyát of Omar Khayyám*. This in my teens.

Later, I would live a mile or two from Edward FitzGerald's grave, where I would sometimes sit and murmur his quatrains. The long poem is heady with wine, friendship, roses, and human dust.

The churchyard was nicely rank. 'It is He that hath made us and not we ourselves', reads the inscription. 'He' had made not only a genius but a very strange man. I made him one of my first literary heroes.

As for my committed-to-memory *Rubáiyát*, it has a habit of falling to pieces in my head these days. Rather like the communion service of an old priest I once served. He prided himself on being able to do without the book, but whole lines from the liturgy had tumbled out of his head, to be picked up by me. 'Ye that do truly and earnestly repent you of your sins . . .' Space . . . then me: 'and are in love and charity with your neighbours . . .' then him. And so on. And nothing said in the vestry; for he then remembered that he had said it all. A good old man, mildly adrift.

At the University of Essex, Marina Warner has involved me in something she calls a 'memory bank'. It involved others, too. We remember things that no one else could. I remembered things about the artist Thomas Gainsborough, having been brought up in his little Suffolk birthplace and caught a drift of him which had never got into books. Marcel Proust, Thomas Hardy, Seamus Heaney, David the Psalmist, John Clare – they each banked the unreliable facts of their youth for future reference, so that they could be invested in classic truths.

Psychiatrists and confessors rifle our memory hoard, turning out the attic junk to leave a clear space. Should they? In Oliver Goldsmith's poem 'The Deserted Village', everyone marvelled that the schoolmaster's little head could contain all that he knew. I see him, like myself, clambering around in its learning to find something useful to say. To write. Like Isaiah or Job, or Jesus, something beautiful to teach. Or to create from.

The snowdrops are remembering to come up, but the oak leaves are forgetting to come down. And the mercifully foxless Essex and Suffolk Hunt is streaming across the fields, and the white cat remembers my safe arms; for the cries of men, women, and beasts shake her universe.

Wild Days

THE BRIEF cold violence of a March storm. All was as usual when a meteorological racket vented itself on our fields for all it was worth. Rain rushed down, winds cut the sky to pieces, lightning blackened and blinded the landscape in turn, thunder split our eardrums. Church towers rocked. Beasts cowered. And then – silence, after which the sound of all sorts of gutters and tracks doing their stuff.

Later, my eyes falling on a medieval gargoyle that now lies inside the church, I thought I saw a look of longing. What a come-down. Once, the March downpour gushed from that gaping mouth for centuries; now, only a concern for archaeology prevents us from stuffing it with our dripping brollies. Its stone lips are worn thin by historic waterfalls. Gargoyles have such sad features as they shoot the rain away from the walls and on to the dead. I give ours a little pat.

Deserts, not rains, are what we are to think about. Yet science has robbed us of their convenient Lenten aridity. No longer can we use them as geographical wastes; for now we know that they teem with life. The three great Abrahamic faiths are seeded in the same desert. Jews, Christians, and Muslims entered human consciousness from the same gritty source. When we follow Christ as best we can into the desert, we enter his dilemma, his privation and terrible decision, and it is no longer a horrifying place.

But deserts do strange things to natural sounds. Voices are not what they seem. Reductive messages blow over the dunes, teasing the human ear. One day, a poet would call the desert's mocking bluff by seeing eternity in a grain of sand.

At the Lenten matins I wait for Christopher to come to Isaiah's prophecy, one that Jesus would have known: 'For the Lord shall comfort Zion: he will comfort all her waste places: and he will make her wilderness like Eden, and her desert like the garden of the Lord; joy and gladness shall be found therein, thanksgiving and the voice of melody.'

May we not now accept this ecologically as well as theologically? You know it makes sense. And of course we sing the 'Benedicite', clustering its praises. The village is chilly and drafty. 'I can't get warm,' says an old neighbour. There is a time when one cannot get warm. It is when one cannot get going as one used to.

But the March sun, once the March winds have stopped blowing it about, is enchanting. I feel it on the back of my neck as I clear the nut-walk, a surprising caress. And there are Easter lambs in Bowden's Lane as usual.

After the service, a visitor asks me to explain the *Agnus Dei* in the east window. Is it something to do with a coat of arms? Well, yes and no.

Gardening again; a lurid sky turns the earth blood-red. I

toil right up to the first lashings of a second squall. The raindrops are huge and flatten my hair. Also the cat's. We enter the house in a dead heat.

The naked trees hurl themselves about; and can that Niagara roar be my downpipe – the one that props up the clematis? And is the roof safe? And the fat brick Tudor chimney that balances the TV aerial on its nose? And do the hosts of Midian prowl and prowl around? It sounds like it.

Two Suffolk Towns

SHAMEFULLY, having mislaid my path in dear familiar Ipswich, I am reduced to asking directions. Three tall ancient men sunning themselves by a wall regard me before answering. They have the thin, polished cheekbones that Suffolk males possessed before modern diet obliterated them.

One of them asks, 'What would you be looking for there?' What indeed. The winner of a new literary prize should be the reply. But I mumble the name of a library. 'Second right up there.' Of course.

The bliss of idleness after the statutory half-century of toil, the indescribable touch of an April sun on old skin. Country towns bring them out, these morning groups. The low murmuring of their talk is like the sound of the mining bees in the bank of my track. 'Poor fool,' they will be telling each other. 'Doesn't know his way to Tavern Street.'

I had been taking Ipswich in, and discovering how fond I

am of it. The Orwell coldly shining, the floor of St Mary-le-Tower glittering like a skating rink, the candy-striped market stalls, the extraordinary number of late-medieval houses, the muddling crowds, the Buttermarket, its airs and graces – all county towns have their airs and graces.

Quite a lot of what I had been seeing is what Wolsey would have seen as a boy. Anne, helping to judge the literary competition, says: 'What I can't understand is why these business types want all this money. I mean, what is the point of it?'

Why did Cardinal Wolsey want so much property, and he a priest? And he a thin Ipswich lad all fattened up to speak for the Church. 'Came a cropper, didn't he,' that old chap by the wall might have remarked. Often all that is remembered about someone is their fall.

Sloe-blossom powders my lane. Mowing, I suddenly think of the Queen singing John Mason's wonderful 'How shall I sing that Majesty which angels do admire?' in which the poet tells God:

Thou art a sea without a shore,
A sun without a sphere;
Thy time is now and evermore,
Thy place is everywhere.

For worship, magnificent or simple, has a way of not ceasing when the service ends, but repeats itself for days afterwards. And so I am still in St Edmundsbury Cathedral, at the royal Maundy service, and the Queen is four lay canons to my right, and the Beefeaters, the Children of the Chapel Royal, and almost a thousand of us are singing this fine seventeenth-century hymn to Coe Fen all over again.

Its author was a strange man – ecstatic at times, but thrilling in the hymn book. And Bury, like Ipswich, was milling with crowds. And, should the sun come out, so would old men, to stand by warm walls and see what was going on, and to give directions. 'All streets are theatres,' I wrote long ago. When your time comes, it could be pleasant to find where it is standing-room only.

Rape is giving the landscape its annual Midas touch. Soon it will be a yellow universe. That is where it is not a silvery-grey world, for horrible plastic preserves acres of crops from late frosts. 'But there you are!' as an old friend used to say.

APRIL

Pangur Bán the Cat

IT HAS been an extraordinary catty kind of day. First, Jamie the postman brought me a fat packet from a treasured friend in Armagh, where, although I have still not visited that holy ground, I am beginning to feel at home, and in which she has included the origins of that great cat poem 'Pangur Bán'.

I first came across it in Seamus Heaney's and Ted Hughes's anthology *The Rattle Bag*. 'Written by a student of the monastery of Carinthia on a copy of St Paul's Epistles in the eighth century', it said. I longed to know more, and then from Armagh came this:

'Writing in the scriptorium was hard work. One monk, from Ireland, has left us a piece of poetry he wrote in the Irish language. This scribe was very glad to have a friendly white cat beside him as he wrote. He saw that the cat also had work to do. The cat hunted mice, while his master, the scribe, hunted words.

'This poem, translated from the old Irish language, is aged a thousand years. The two words Pangur and Bán both mean "white". Pangur Bán must have been a very white cat indeed.'

I and Pangur Bán, my cat,

'Tis a like task we are at;
Hunting mice is his delight,
Hunting words I sit all night.

. . . So in peace our tasks we ply,
Pangur Bán, my cat, and I;
In our arts we find our bliss,
I have mine and he has his.

No room for the entirety of this fine cat poem. I read it to
my white cat, who is dozing on the notes for chapter three.
Bliss is certainly obvious, but when did she last hunt a
mouse? Whiter than white, like Pangur Bán, she opens an
eye to remind me that the Middle Ages were plagued not
only by knights, priests, dames, the poor, etc., but by mice.
Also – no Whiskas.

They had their rewards, however; for a hard-hunting cat
could be 'sung' by poets, or get itself pictured in stained
glass, as in the Julian window in Norwich Cathedral.

Practice every day has made
Pangur perfect in his trade;
I get wisdom day and night
Turning darkness into light.
[By which I assume he means translating St Paul into
Gaelic.]

It is at this scholarly moment that Tom Cox appears, to give
me his book *Under the Paw: Confessions of a cat man*. Tom
is tall, dark and thin, and looks as though he had just
escaped the denouement of a D. H. Lawrence story. He

gives the white cat a knowing glance. He and his wife have six cats. They live in darkest Norfolk. I mean to introduce him there and then to Pangur Bán, but we devour cake and talk about long walks, and how many words we have written today.

After he has disappeared, I read *Under the Paw* in the hot April garden. It is absurd, enchanting. Tom's aim is to name a star after his best cat.

The Royal Maundy and the Badgers

SPRING again. Holy Week once more. A hot sun and a cold wind. Plus 'The uncertain glory of an April day' (William Shakespeare). The grass having sprung, I give it the first mow of the year, and the garden is pulled together.

Countless flowers – never were there so many. And a few bees. And an orchestrated woodland of birds. Marsh marigolds are cupped over frogspawn in the old horse-pond. The clouds are sumptuous, banking, riding high. When in 1913 Igor Stravinsky presented his throbbing ballet *Rite of Spring*, there was public agitation. Spring was supposed to be a time when prettiness hid earthiness.

Nothing can hide the shocking events of Holy Week, however: the arrest, the trial, the desertion of friends, the selflessness of women, the ancient rite of Passover. And thus the world should have moved on. Execution requires that it should.

In St Edmundsbury Cathedral, the Queen distributes the Royal Maundy money. I watch her distantly from my lay canon's stall, the small figure passing slowly from recipient to recipient, the clergy richly sombre, the music flowing. Soon it is done. In the distance, I glimpse familiar Suffolk faces and (I fancy) medieval pilgrims. And rings of light. I have had to use my passport to get into this event, just to prove that I am OK.

Maundy – *mandatum novum* – 'A new commandment I give unto you, that you love one another.' All this to be repeated in the evening at Wormingford – sans the money, of course. And then I shall help strip the altar – our faith's spring rite.

Between these sacred rituals, I may have time to sow some potatoes. Perhaps in a hoed trench, and not with the dib. I will lay them out in a row like a string of shooting beads, and the birds will holler and the grass walks will look handsome.

Beautiful towns tumble down on the news; for God was not in the earthquake. Tectonic plates shift. Spring is so beautiful in central Italy, but nature is not confined to the surface. What a Holy Week!

At home already rich people claim expenses. Why is it that they need so much money, must have every pound due to them? As children, we would cry, 'That's mine! That's mine!' But we grew out of it – some of us at least. Simply because we couldn't see the point of it, this claiming, this declaring our rights.

Some politicians' expense lists are too vulgar to think about, and one only hopes that their exposure will shame them. There is a well-known disease of corn called Take-all. It is a fungus that blights growth and contaminates a field. 'Take all if it is your due,' say some. But why?

A spring day is for visitation, and so I call on the badgers and clamber down the boundary ditch to see how the wild garlic is getting on. The badgers are sound asleep, and the garlic smells good. I rake in some poppy seeds from last year. I mis-identify birdsong, this being my least best subject.

I take friends up to Little Cornard to show them where Martin Shaw set 'Hills of the North, rejoice!' It is part of my boyhood country, and although the three of us do not shout as we journey on, we do feel an exultancy on this rural height. 'What a day!' we repeat. 'What a day!'

There are scattered farms and apple orchards and bumpy tracks. And Sudbury like Jerusalem in the distance.

Pastoral Imagery

EACH YEAR, I alternate the Sundays after Easter with sermons on Emmaus and the image of the Lamb. So this year it is Shepherd Sunday, the divine pastoral. All week, expensive altar lilies have been trumpeting their deathliness, and a sumptuous mortality fills the nave. Nothing can approach the liturgical sequence of odours in a country church.

A news item rocks – wrecks – what I have to say, however. The Sophoclean tragedy of Katyn. And that this should have been staged in Poland, the most Christian nation in Europe. So what to say? Say nothing. Say: 'Let us remember Poland in silence before God.' Which we do, and at both matins and evensong. During the latter, a great tit sang clearly and repetitively near by. For Poland, an appalling crime, one of the worst in history, would in future be overlaid with a banal crash.

On Easter Two the Gospel is – or was – 'Jesus said, I am the good shepherd: the good shepherd giveth his life for the sheep.' The creature most identified with our faith is the lamb. Suffolks are pastured in the meadow below St Andrew's, leaping, crying, thrusting against their mothers in the cold April air. And in what would become Palestine, a tribe of herdsmen, always moving on to fresh grass, would eventually settle and produce shepherd-kings.

The lambs have children's voices when they cry, which can be unsettling. How at our mercy they are, these Christ-symbolizing animals. How can we escape the questions they pose? Living creature, altar symbol, the Word.

It was the Lord's cousin, John, who challenged the old lamb-sacrificing religion by calling out in his grown-up voice, 'Behold the Lamb of God!' The paschal lamb provided a feast. It was sacrificed in the temple on the afternoon of 14 Nisan, or mid-April, ritually offered to God, then taken home and eaten for supper. All this to remind a pastoral nation of its freedom from servitude.

St Paul is referring to this when he tells his Corinth friends: 'Christ our passover is sacrificed for us, therefore let us keep the feast. Not with the old leaven, nor with the leaven of malice and wickedness, but with the unleavened bread of sincerity and truth.'

What does the Lamb himself say, this second Sunday after Easter? 'I am the good shepherd who gave his life so that you can live. I never ran away when the sacrificial moment came. I am constancy. You left me. But now you are returned to the shepherd and bishop (overseer) of your souls.'

'No sheepdogs in the Bible,' David says. His has been in the pond, and is scattering water over us. The white cat, used to him by now, sits cautiously aloft all the same.

After the pastoral people stopped wandering, their shepherds still had to lead their flocks from feeding-ground to feeding-ground on the hills, making pens, fires, and, inevitably, poems. For when you lie dreaming on your back under the stars, you think of the strangest, most beautiful things. Which is how we got the Psalms. And the names for the stars. And mystics. And writers such as Thomas Traherne and Richard Rolle.

The Baptist by the River

YESTERDAY, the Bishop of Colchester arrived to confirm four young people at Mount Bures. Spring rain. Spring sunshine. Everyone dressed up and looking rather beautiful. Six churchwardens from our three parishes walk before the Bishop, and I, as his chaplain, trail behind him. A slow, majestic parade to 'Lord of the Dance'. A Perpendicular western window lets in downpour-light and sunlight. The grass has been lawned for the first time.

We are in the bailey of a Norman castle, the sacred corner of it. The motte itself has grown a mop of tall trees and bushes, so that it is impossible for a sentry to look out over the Colne valley to see if anyone is coming. We are confined by rubble and Roman tiles.

I read the story about Dorcas the dressmaker, and Henry the Rector serves the Bishop at the eucharist, and I try not to get in their way. Ritual tends to make me dream.

Confirmed, new, the first communicants hold out their hands and take the big silver cup, after which arrive the familiar hands I have seen for half a lifetime, hardly any as rough as they once were; for who touches the soil these rural days? The Bishop is unhurried, almost still, yet at the same time ceaselessly active. It is a great gift.

How curious it is, this sameness, this difference, this freshness of April flowers, this usage of old things, old language, old feelings, and their refusal to wear out. Glass reflections travel over memorials and people's faces, pure blue, dramatic red. Over the formalities of the visiting choir. Over the snowy wafers.

A rustic Baptist, perched semi-naked on the corner of the reredos like someone who must burst in on ritual, catches the Bishop's eye. Afterwards I explain. During the last war, farmer Brown lost his son, a fighter-pilot and very young, during the Battle of Britain. So he had an artist carve his lasting Voice. Eventually, John's stick fell from his hand, and tumbled to dust. So another John, who worked in the seed-shed at Arger Fen, cut him a fresh one that should see us all out.

The Bishop absorbs this fragment of local history – 'It is enough.' Also, he has to repeat this poetic performance at Lawford later today, measuring out his quiet words, being serious, being memorable. Lawford is estuarial. It is where the Stour broadens into shallows, into sea-like depths, and through whose muddy-river lanes John Constable waded to sketch Nelson's *Victory*. It is a sopping-wet world of swans and reflections, arrivals and departures, far cries and close encounters.

St John's voice carried by the Jordan as a herald's should. I hear it as a youthful shout, clear as a trumpet. The bigwigs ask who gave him permission to wake the dead – waken the government. Who was he, anyway? 'I am a voice crying in the wilderness, "Prepare the way!"' People went to watch him, not hear him, to his Lord's annoyance. His river was about the same size as ours. Poets would feed its currents, open out its source, be carried away on its divine passage to the eternal harbour.

Ritual can kill faith, or recreate it. I think we did the latter. In fact, I am sure we did: else I would not be so haunted by what happened last Sunday.

Mrs Cardy

NOW IS the time to praise great countrywomen. Both Rosa and Mary were to endure those protracted last days that are now the norm of long lives. Each knew the greatness of small things.

Rosa Cardy was, among other disappearing professions, needlewoman to a country-house. Mary Newcomb was a wonderful artist, who saw what most of us, with our clogged vision, would not have noticed had she not pointed it out to us.

Rosa sang in the church choir for maybe some 80 years, with perfect pitch, an elegant little figure for whom the service was never routine, never humdrum, but something beautiful to do on Sundays. She had been baptized, married, and celebrated in this ancient building above the Stour. It was, as with numberless Wormingford people, a reliquary containing her inner life.

Her outer existence was everywhere, in village terms. She was a woman who took part. Not to take part used to be a severe form of criticism. Nowadays, a good half of a rural parish is not only unlikely to take part, but also likely to stay invisible.

Villages were, until recently, divided between the newcomers and the 'old people'; the latter were not aged necessarily, but rooted. Rosa was rooted. She and her husband the horseman went back for centuries.

Horsemen is what we in East Anglia called our ploughmen. I see, in my imagination, Mr Cardy going up and down, up and down our hilly fields, a long time ago. I also see Rosa taking part in the Dramatic Society's productions. One would have needed to have an unusual negative ability to stay out of these, even more so if one's face fitted a particular role.

The Society was dominated, or shall we say led, by Christine Nash, the wife of the artist John Nash, and by Guy Hickson, the brother of Joan Hickson, aka Miss Marple. And there, in many black-and-white stills, stands or sits Rosa. And now, aged almost 100, she has gone.

At her funeral, I told the packed church what they already knew; for this is what country mourners expect. Her small coffin had been set between myself and the vicar on tall trestles. Her favourite hymn was Joseph Addison's 'When all thy mercies, O my God, my rising soul surveys', with its courageous philosophy.

Something I did long ago occurred to me as I gazed on her flowers. Writers being daydreamers, I had missed out a bit of the liturgy. Should I go on, or back-track? I went on. From across the chancel I felt rather than saw Mrs Cardy looking at me reproachfully, her gentle recognition of the imperfection of human nature, especially a writer's human nature, all too apparent. I had taken something from her.

Mary Newcomb would have drawn her – would have recorded her quietness. It would not be too extravagant for us to admit that before certain artists, composers, and writers arrived in our midst, we were unable to see what was most familiar to us, our local landscape, or, indeed, ourselves.

Mary walked and biked her way through sparse Suffolk scenes that contained glories that we could never have known had she not shown them to us. There is much human idling in her paintings, much going nowhere. And a tumbling beach café with a couple of locals will disconcertingly give out as much illumination as the lighthouse, though of another sort.

She draws bird meditation, although this has nothing to do with bird-watching. She once said that 'she exchanged words with the occupants of a landscape'. It was hard to exchange words with a ploughman. You got them in on the turn – as in Edward Thomas's great wartime poem.

The General Thanksgiving

RETURNING from Mary's funeral feast at the Thatcher's Arms, we see Mark drilling. Today's thin April rain and yesterday's warm April sun give a two-tone surface to the seed-bed. The drill doesn't have to miss Shoals, the saucer dip, which would have been a shallow pond when Mary was a girl; for it is now as dry as the rest of the field. No slough of despond in these days.

The machine makes a welcome clatter and drone. Nesting birds are noisy. At the funeral, we said the General Thanksgiving. 'This to be said when any that have been prayed for desire to return praise.'

A fervent rumble of 'We bless thee for our creation, preservation, and all the blessings of this life; but above all for thine inestimable love' had filled the old church, as we all stood, or rather crouched, proxy for Mary in gratitude. She had been a woman of beautiful language, of surprising words, who had very nearly seen her century out. The church had been heady with Easter flowers.

I change and drag the lawnmower out into the light for its first cut. The grass is rich and tall. A friend – a great gardener – deplored today's fashion of cutting it all the year. 'Don't forget it is a plant,' he would say, 'and it needs to grow.' To put down this year's roots. To wave a bit. What was Mark drilling, we wonder – sugar beet? His drill climbs up the hill, passes the badgers' sett, and wanders away into an inestimable distance, pencilling the spring earth.

It is a perfect moment for fecundity. We need not bother God with the prayer for plenty, or with thanks for it either, as Mark's seeds make themselves at home in their shallow rut. The garden has got a head start on them and is crowded with blooms, wild and tamed. Patches of new grass are spared the lawnmower as they are rich with celandine and violets.

The General Thanksgiving was written by Edward Reynolds in 1661, the year he became Bishop of Norwich, and was called thus to differentiate it from the particular thanksgivings for rain, fair weather, peace, etc. The thanksgiving for health is ignorant of medicine, and views sickness as a divine visitation 'for our sins' and takes us into a world of fear and retribution, superstition, and helplessness. But as someone associated with sensible Puritan Norwich, and an excellent writer, I like to think that corn-growing East Anglia entered Bishop Reynolds's mind when he created the General Thanksgiving, which remains adequate for our general awareness of being looked after by our creator.

Bottengoms Farm benefits from the February coppicing. The morning sun floods it. It is warm on my back as I sit at the desk. It – and the rain – hits the old house. One can easily get grown in. Half a dozen years, and the shadows fall. There are heavy spring dews, the kind that John Constable dared to paint with Chinese white, to the hilarity of the Royal Academy. It believed that green fields and trees were all right for the countryside but were not at all right for Art. Brown for framed grass. And when the great artist painted dew – 'Constable's snowstorm' – it didn't know whether to laugh or rage. But there it is, shining on every leaf, my April brilliance.

MAY

Norfolk and Ithaca

COLD MAY mornings. None the less, the white cat has deserted the warm kitchen for a mossy wall. There she lies, smelling bluebells, hearing larks, imagining – what? Best not to ask. We ask, of course, since it is Rogation.

Once upon a time, and in another place, the harmonium was roped to the apple cart and played round the parish, all of us trailing behind. We sang 'Eternal Ruler of the ceaseless round' to Orlando Gibbons by the pond in which our Baptists were baptized. Only years ago. Now, we process through park-like gardens, though ending up in the churchyard all the same. After which comes Matthias, who filled Judas's place by the luck of the draw. A strangely beautiful week, filled with light and obscurities.

The orchard grass grows with a shaggy richness, and the pear blossom is sumptuous. But it is chilly, and I sow vegetables wearing an old jersey. I do my accounts for the accountant, a miserable business. Chickens in the shape of wild transactions come home to roost. What a lot of food I have eaten. As for books and socks and Whiskas and subs and gin . . . What a good thing that I have forgotten how to add up.

The Gospels chink with small change, mites, and Roman pennies, their wealth being of another kind. Christ made little of money and sex, but his Church made much of both. On and on it goes, counting, discounting, when it should be listening to circling planets singing on their way; for life on this one is short and should be glorious. Will He not ask us: 'Why didn't you enjoy it more – my earth?' And we will answer: 'We would have done, but there were all these blessed accounts.'

To Wells-next-the-Sea for the poetry festival. Winds play along the Norfolk coast. The poets and their audiences assemble. I have to do something called 'Desert Island Readings' with Kevin Crossley-Holland at midday. The North Sea glitters, and, having come so far, I have a fancy to go on to the Wash. But I must come home for Rogation and a lesser journey.

Kevin is a fine translator of Anglo-Saxon poems, a restless literature from a people who took ages to settle down. It was 'Get the boat out!' just when they should be farming. Vast waters called them. Until the Celtic saints brought them cheering news, they were very depressed as a race. One of my desert-island readings is Constantine Cavafy's 'Ithaca'. Its theme is that it is better to travel than to arrive.

Always have Ithaca at the back of your mind.
The arrival there is your objective.
But do not be in any hurry on your journey.
Better to let it last for years.
In old age you will anchor at the island,
Rich with all you have gained upon the way,
Not expecting Ithaca to give you riches.
Ithaca gave you the lovely journey.

Without her you would not have started –
But she has nothing more to give you . . .

Queen Esther and the Roadmen

'DID YOU know that there are only two readings from the
Book of Esther?' asked the churchwarden. Really? Back
home, I reread this sumptuous but sorry tale about the
lovely Queen Vashti, sent packing because she refused to be
a beauty queen at her husband's party, and the lovely
Queen Esther, her successor, who was able to prevent an
early holocaust against her people, the Jews. It all took place
in countries we now call Iraq and Iran.

The splendours and barbarities have not changed a bit,
for such is life. Lots of wine, lots of love, lots of hangings.
Xerxes (here called Ahasuerus), Vashti, Esther, her uncle
Mordecai the Jew, and Haman the Nazi are operatic figures,
although also People of Today.

No one quotes the Book of Esther in the New Testament,
and no wonder. No one in the Book of Esther mentions
God. It is a great read. 'The drinking was according to
the law' which said, 'Drink as much or as little as you like'.
The King's heart was usually merry with wine. Here
was born the Jewish festival of Purim, a springtime feast.
Thus a divine poetry sprang from these all-too-worldly
weaknesses.

When an interesting new plant arrives, it can be
temporarily heeled-in while one finds a permanent home
for it – an all-sun place, and with the kind of neighbour it

61

can get on with for ages to come. Needless to say, this spot is occupied by much rubbish.

The plant is a round-leaf sage from Perigord. It takes an hour to clear the spot, dig it deep, and trim back the sage's companion, a raggedy old rosemary which I planted in memory of my friend Victoria, a botanical artist. But what suitable earth. The sage takes to it like Perigord earth, not wilting, and, finally, when I have done all the raking and petting, like it has never been anywhere else. I am so pleased with it that I keep on visiting it. It smells French.

Roadmen are mending the lane. 'Leaning on their spades,' says a woman. But there are no spades, and the men, six of them, work hard. Their white hats and yellow coats burn in the sun. There are five different tar and roll vehicles, and harsh diversion signs. Ditches which would have taken two men a month to clear are restored in an hour. Drains are inserted, holes patched. The postman cannot reach me.

Friends in cars panic on their mobiles. 'How can we get to you?' They are all of a mile away. 'It is a nice walk,' I suggest. I cannot be serious.

The road that is being patched up is waterlogged in winter. It winds in extravagant loops to the church, with a tractor or a 4×4 round every bend. The men have trimmed its edge so that tarmac peters into dirt and the flints gathered by women and children long ago shine. It is hung with wild roses. The patching is an inch below the surface, so presumably we may hope for one of those black sheets which issue from a machine like toothpaste.

I prepare my talk for the Aldeburgh Festival. It is about rural writing in the twentieth century. The first years, with their ruined farms and flocks of casual workers, and still remote communities, were a gift to my teenage heroes H. E. Bates and A. E. Coppard. Should I take a collection of their short stories from the shelf, my heart will be as merry as Xerxes's.

Shandy Hall

MORE GADDING. I have longed for ages to see my friend Patrick Wildgust, the curator of Shandy Hall in faraway Yorkshire. And now I am there, alongside other devotees of Laurence Sterne, Perpetual Curate of Coxwold and author of *Tristram Shandy* and *A Sentimental Journey*. The latter title suits me admirably.

Shandy Hall is so exactly as I imagined it that it is like running into Emily Brontë on the moor. Except that, as Haworth is the very spirit of *Wuthering Heights*, so Shandy Hall is still so as the Revd Laurence Sterne left it in the 1760s that I expected to find him weeding. Instead, Patrick gallops out to see me in.

A young man plays a viola da gamba in the panelled parlour. Swallows zoom in and out of the stable. Purple clouds hang over Byland Abbey. Polished, worn stairs take me to my room, the same stairs that Sterne climbed, the same rail that prevented him from sliding down.

I unpack my clean shirt and my sermon, which is the one on the Walking Christ which I take around with me, adding this and that. The accounts of Sterne's preaching do not agree. Some biographers say that half the congregation left the minute he began to speak; others say that at Coxwold one could not get a seat. Certainly, his sermons broke through what was expected. One on the Prodigal Son advocated the advantages of foreign travel.

In the morning, the Shandy Hall party walked the few steps to St Michael's, which is very beautiful and which only recently received Sterne's body plus his London tombstone.

Many literary priests – Robert Herrick was one – resented being stuck in their rural livings, but Sterne loved his. Yorkshire seems to have accepted his notoriety with ease. He was the master of sentiment, for whom the raffish and the delicate, or the humane, if you like, not to mention a delight in wit, could be put on the page. Even in the notes for the Sunday sermon.

I borrowed the curate's cassock, and preached from Laurence Sterne's triple-decker pulpit. The May sun glinted through the medieval glass. We had listened to my favourite Isaiah verses being perfectly read, and had sung the St Francis hymn. Ian, the young Vicar, had found some fine walking prayers. Folk had arrived from far and wide.

Outside, the steep churchyard ran down to a stream. There was a big dandelion square, containing a soldier who had charged in the Light Brigade. His grave, in all the wide churchyard, lay unmown. Sterne's was sideways on by the south wall, and could not have been more wryly accounted for had he himself written it.

He died from consumption in a room above a silk-bag shop in Old Bond Street in 1768. He was 55. He was buried in St George's new burial ground, and promptly dug up by resurrection men and sold to the medical school in

Cambridge, where it was recognized by a famous physician and returned to Paddington for reburial.

There, two larky freemasons erected a tombstone that began, 'Alas, poor Yorick'. On 4 June 1969, Sterne's body was once again exhumed, because a developer wished to build a block of flats where he lay, and was returned to his loved Coxwold. Hilarious, unique in literature, he had once written: 'I am positive I have a soul: nor can all the books with which materialists have pestered the world ever convince me of the contrary.'

That evening, Patrick, Paul the artist, and the viola da gamba boy and I drove to Byland Abbey in the rain.

Bees, Rabbits, Blythes

IT IS A GREAT moment. David is taking me to Creeting St Mary to see the meadow saxifrage, *Saxifraga granulata*. It will blanket the churchyard. I will also tread native territory, for next door in Creeting St Peter lie generations of Blythe-Blyth-Bly-Bligh ancestors (parsons' spelling).

This is High Suffolk, and, on a good day, you can see Norfolk. Also, in Creeting St Mary church, there is a tender St Christopher inscribed 'Whoever looks at the picture of S. Christopher shall assuredly on that day be burdened with no weariness', and having driven along the A12 on the Spring Bank Holiday we need to give it a glance.

But both Creeting churches are locked, and the St Mary churchyard is rabbit-wrecked. A tragic business. A putto dabs his eyes on an exquisitely sad early gravestone, and no wonder. Where have all the meadow saxifrages gone? Into rabbits' tummies. David is bereft. 'Once,' he says, 'they were such a sight that they made a page-spread photo in the *East Anglian Daily Times*.' We find just one or two flowers waving in the rabbit-churned turf.

Then on to the other Creeting, home of the Blythe-Blyth-Bly-Blighs. A warm wind shakes the unmutilated limes, and cyclists the door-handle. The churchyard itself is still and pensive. Very beautiful.

In his monumental *Flora Britannica*, Richard Mabey says: 'The churchyard has also become a sanctuary for plants. At a time when unimproved grassland has all but disappeared across much of agricultural Britain, these small patches of turf – "God's acres" – are in many parishes the last refuge for species such as meadow saxifrage, green-winged orchid and hoary plantain . . . and were also centres where medicinal herbs were cultivated.'

Beneath the cool May grass in Creeting St Peter churchyard lies 'a herbalist'. Our contribution to churchyard treasure is the harebells, *Campanulaceae rotundifolia* in the plant-rich sward of St John the Baptist, Mount Bures. They appear in the autumn, delicate almost beyond description, where the mower cannot catch them; witch flowers, and not to be picked. Hares are bewitched. But the harebells' blueness! It is only to be matched by that of a child's eye.

Hugh the vet leans from his car to tell me gloomily that he has bees in his chimney, so what to do? Harold, our bee man, is now 90 and past looking after us. A few years ago, he magically called down a swarm from the nave, luring it through the door to a more practical roost. His empty beehives tilt in the long grass.

Antony, my priest friend in the north, has lost his bees in the current bee decline. What is killing Britain's bees? Who doesn't know that we cannot live if the bees die? Scripture has a great deal to say about honey, but not much about the creatures that produce it, the few references being on the hitting-about side – except, of course, the marvellous one in Judges, which Tate & Lyle put on their treacle tin.

The Baptist's meat was wild honey. 'Have you any meat?' asked the risen Christ, and they gave him some broiled fish and a piece of honeycomb. Then they all walked to Bethany, where he parted from them so as never to leave them. Or us. That sweet mystery.

What will the Creeting bees do if the Creeting rabbits devour all the saxifrage? Go to the golden rape fields, I expect. They sprawl to Diss.

A Stranger did Once Bless the Earth

SURVEYING Mammon from the ivory tower of a remote old farmhouse, I am startled more by its incompetence than by its wickedness. Hustled from the boardroom burrow, it blinks feebly in the light of day. One by one, it is asked to state its qualifications for running a vast bank, rather as an Edwardian gardener was required to state his qualifications, and each in turn muttered that he had none. It was frosty theatre. Had William Hazlitt been present, how the sparks would have flown!

Glancing at history, I see yet again that humanity has suffered as much if not more at the hands of the incompetent as by the politically criminal. In the White House, a Daniel really has come to judgment.

Back here at the Stour Valley ranch, for centuries 'out' of history in any monetary sense, and just jogging along, the bankers stare into the old rooms with trapped faces. To think that it has come to this! they might be saying. But who knows? Not the rich young man who was advised to become poor to save his soul.

I am writing about the more or less penniless John Clare, whose publishers have sent him a dateless 'Student's Journal' in which they hope he will make notes for a natural history book rather like that written by Gilbert White. It has no printed dates; so Clare can start it in September.

He is ravished by its paper. Being prolific, he has never possessed nearly enough paper for his needs. Those who could well afford to do so never think of giving him a ream or two. Instead, they give him advice. And when finally he collapsed, the Lunacy Board put it down to covering too much paper.

Before this tragedy, Clare got out. He walked the fields and woods. He socialized in the pub. He would, on a fine day, lie low, and, out of the eye of the labouring world, would be out sensuously watching butterflies, or sniffing wild flowers. Sometimes with a girl.

Those who understood money doled out his slender royalties in case he blued them all at once. The seasons passed; the Glinton bells rang; the new profitable farming wrecked his village; the boardrooms had him in mind. Having read and met Hazlitt, he refused to stick to poetry, and now and then went into the economy-protest business, showing more knowledge of money than he was entitled to – not to say nerve.

The clear white pages of the 'Student's Journal' grew dark with ink. Sometime or other, feeling low, he also felt like someone else. Someone who had a great deal more to say about money than about sex. Finding a sad hymn by another author, he wound himself in it:

A stranger did once bless the earth
Who never caused a heart to mourn,
Whose very voice gave sorrow mirth,
And how did earth his worth return?
It spurned him from his lowliest lot:
The meanest station owned him not.

To be sung to 'Surrey'. And sung by Ted Hughes and myself, and crowds of other people, when we placed a memorial to this 'tenant of the fields' in Poets' Corner.

How to Pray

THERE ARE moments when I need not ask for anything, everything being present. Such as listening to the dawn chorus on a May morning, and with the cold air entering the ancient window in thrilling, quiet power. And having gone to sleep with my nightingale in full voice just outside.

Some of the first Christians were worried by the glories

of nature and went to unnatural lengths to block them out. On the radio, the Thought for the Day man, still a bit delirious from listening to birdsong and Messiaen, is describing exactly what I am thinking at this moment – that prayer is a kind of bliss. Surprisingly, in the Gospels it is an art that has to be learnt, the Teacher and his pupils being young Jews accustomed to synagogue and Temple services.

But Matthew has Jesus telling them to pray on their own and to shut the door; and Mark has him hiding away in the countryside in order to pray. Luke has him being asked that astonishing thing, 'Lord, teach us how to pray.' Thus his prayer, which became the foundation of public worship, was originally intended for the solitary place. This particular spring day my morning prayer is being set to music by birdsong, as had the speaker's on the radio.

George Herbert, as one would expect of a priest, puts public prayer first, although being unable to resist confessing the enchantments of private prayer. The latter are frequently quoted; the former rarely. But we would do well to read what he said; for it might improve our services. How I dislike the barked-out responses. Here is what Herbert said.

Though private prayer be a brave design,
Yet publick hath more promises, more love:
And love's a weight to hearts, to eies a signe.
We all are but cold suitours; let us move
Where it is warmest. Leave thy six and seven;
Pray with the most: for where most pray, is heaven.

But, although I have no proof of it, I am convinced that Herbert's wildly happy and celebrated analysis of what prayer is to him personally comes from a private experience.

> Softnesse, and peace, and joy, and love, and blisse,
> Exalted manna, gladnesse of the best,
> Heaven in ordinarie, man well drest,
> The Milkie Way, the bird of Paradise.

The 'ordinarie' was the public table in an inn – Suffolk farmers ate together at the 'ordinary' of a pub on market-day when I was a boy. And 'man well drest' was Herbert remembering his dandy days at Cambridge. What leaps his private prayer took!

The disciples were remembering how John the Baptist taught prayer when they asked Jesus to teach them. John was an outsider where public worship was concerned, and I like to imagine that, as with the Celtic church, his prayer language was a personal one which, when spoken in the open air in what I sense was a glorious voice, might have accompanied birdsong, and wind and river sounds.

How the Nightingale Sings

'I CANNOT bear it!' laments the old friend.

We are waiting in the parked car while the market-day crowd mills around us, packed country buses grind through the ancient streets, stalls are packing up, and the borough arms whip from the town hall mast. They depict a

71

murdered Archbishop of Canterbury's little dog on a crimson ground. Thomas Gainsborough, a native, straddles his plinth, palette at the ready. Plaster labourers loll against sheaves on the Corn Exchange.

I know what the old friend cannot bear; for she has told me many times. Briefly, it is that one day, even soon, she will not be here, and everyone else will. Women will be buying lipsticks and scent at the cosmetic counter, bananas will be sold off as the tarpaulin is dragged from the framework, the golden church-clock will tell a time that she will not experience.

Did I suffer a similar unbearable thought? I said that it was a common one, but, no, to be honest, I did not. Time-wise, I hardly knew where I stood, being a kind of daily person. 'Neither look back nor forward,' advised Jesus, 'or you will miss today.' Generally speaking, I would not miss today for anything.

Amid the mayhem of the *Today* programme, I hear that the essay is making a comeback. Being a chronic essayist, I make more toast as a sign of approval.

Long ago, I wrote a book on William Hazlitt, our Montaigne. An essay means to assay, to go forth, usually rather recklessly; to keep a subject in the air as thought follows thought. He was a great racquet-player on the St Martin's Street court – where the public library now stands – and a dab hand at keeping a ball in the air.

When his essays began to be published in the *Morning Chronicle* in 1812, his enemies were terrified. Where might not his truthfulness fall? He, of course, acknowledged his master, Montaigne. 'In taking up his pen, he did not set up for a philosopher, wit, orator, or moralist, but he became all these by merely daring to tell us whatever passed through his mind.'

All the best essayists give us a piece of their minds in brief, brilliant helpings. Jesus gave us his mind in pithy statements, short stories, and recovered truths.

A nightingale is singing in the garden. His family home is Tiger Hill, about four miles distant, but he sings somewhere beyond the ash tree, his measured voice 'A liquid wheet, a loud tac, a soft, very short tuc, and a harsh kerr of alarm. His song is rich, loud, and musical, each note rapidly repeated several times; most characteristic notes, a deep bubbling chook-chook-chook and a slow piu, piu, piu rising to a brilliant crescendo. Sings day and night from deep cover . . . lowland woods, moist thickets, tangled hedges . . .'

All this from my beloved Collins *Field Guide to the Birds of Britain and Europe*. The white cat listens, too, snowy in the darkness. John Keats, like my friend, was desolated by the thought that this bird would be singing when he could no longer hear it. He said that it was not born for death; yet it was. Though not its song, or his song.

The Lord puzzled his friends. He must die in order that he could 'live'? The spring sunshine would have warmed their faces. All around them, life was going on – would go on, this being its nature.

JUNE

Stroke Ward

VISITING HOURS. Six old men lie in the 'Stroke ward', as a neighbour calls it. The ward is new, but not bright. It is where it is always late afternoon, even before lunch. The atmosphere is serene, or maybe lifeless. One old heart-man – my hospital-going neighbour again – watches the cricket. The television hangs before his face like a vast clock, ticking away with runs.

The patient who holds my attention lies in the foetal position that would naturally be the last one we would assume before religion laid us out from east to west. He is wispy, child-size, faintly breathing through a mask. Every now and then he tries to rid himself of the foreign thing on his face, and his grandson prevents it.

The grandson, son, and the daughter who has just flown in as fast as she could after hearing about the stroke are big, suntanned creatures in shorts, bursting, as they say, with health. Also problematic; for how could this wisp have begotten them? 'Dad, Dad,' repeats the large lady, sorrowfully. There can be no response.

An elegant Asian doctor rattles the curtain around the familiar scene without speaking, and then, five minutes later, presents the final act. It is one of beauty and order. The dying man is propped against a mountain of pillows.

He has a fine face. His children are composed, and will not go away.

I think of George Herbert on that final Bemerton morning, driving his noisily weeping family from his room so that they would not see his joy.

Visiting hours in the care home are anything one likes to make them, within reason. More clean stairs, more intimate glimpses of profound happenings to strangers. The old friend is regal in the armchair brought from the delightful house. She is tall and thin, well-dressed, jewelled, and 92. All the care-home furniture has been moved out, and replaced with that from home. Her late husband's portrait and some other paintings hang on the walls. She is witty, cannot walk, cannot abide unchilled sherry. 'Look, Christina,' says the Polish boy, 'I have filled it to the brim for you.'

'They are all lovely,' she says when he has gone – these helpers, or whatever one has to call them. The fees! The beautiful house is on the market, but something has happened to her in that she no longer cares – 'Don't give a damn, dear.' We eat dark chocolates.

I preach on public and private prayer. What a strange thing for his disciple to ask, 'Teach us how to pray, Lord,' when, as a Jew, he would have been praying on and off all day and every day. But he had seen what the prayer had not intended him to see, Himself alone. Could the prayer that Christ prayed alone be that which he taught us? But for Him in the singular?

Herbert adored forsaking petitionary prayer for conversational prayer. Such talk between him and his Friend! He did not mind becoming absurd in describing it – the analogies tumbling over each other, 'the soul in paraphrase, a kind of tune, Heaven in ordinary [on market days the Suffolk farmers had lunch together at the "ordinary table" in the hotel], the bird of Paradise, church-bells beyond the stars . . .'

And then, coming down to earth, prayer of this kind was simply something understood. No more, no less.

Long Melford

COLIN, carrying Louis, his new son, who is 20 months old, shouts through the hedge. Having come back from New Zealand yesterday, how can they have plunged through the tall pre-haymaking grass so soon?

Louis is beautiful beyond words, and clearly still trailing those clouds of glory whence he came. Colin is tanned and bristly. I stand amazed at Louis. Colin says, 'I used to look like him.' How could that be?

No, they haven't jet-lag. Colin, a master book-conservator, has been mending ancient volumes for the Australian government, although one would have thought that none of them could have been old enough to warrant his expertise.

How am I to celebrate his homecoming and my first sight of Louis? Were we in a Barbara Pym novel, we would break open a tin of pilchards and make an extra strong cup of Nescafé. But we have a glass of red wine which makes us dizzy at this time of the morning.

Louis swigs two glasses of orangeade. He closes his eyes as he drinks, resting them on the rim. 'He will not remember this,' I say. 'No, he won't,' says Colin. But I will – always. The blazing day, the drenching scent of the roses, and Colin and his family home at the farm safe and sound. And the white cat dozing on a mat of stone crop not far from the lovely child.

Another day. We take a look at Long Melford fair, just up the road. It is afternoon, when roundabouts and swings sleep. When the gaudy clamour is silent. When the mysterious fair-folk hide in their trailers. The amusements are static, and huddle against a Tudor wall. Not all that much time ago, this was the mighty horse-fair, which, for centuries, competed with the mystery of the Holy Trinity. Its 'priests' were the Romanies who came from near and far. Its writers and artists included George Borrow and Alfred Munnings. This was the domain of *Romany Rye* and *Lavengro*. The windows of the surrounding houses were boarded up against the fights. The naphtha lights glittered on the miraculous church. The unparalleled fair music churned out for hours on the summer green.

We go to the curiously independent Lady chapel to savour its cool interior. It is locked – 'Long Melford fair', explains a kind soul. Inside the main building, all the lords and ladies of East Anglia shake their glass heads – Long Melford fair . . . They are a glass portrait gallery of the late Middle Ages, and if you want to understand their Catholic universe you must read Eamon Duffy's marvellous *The Stripping of the Altars: Traditional Religion in England 1400–1580.*

When I biked to the fair as a boy, I used to wander up to the church to look at what these glass people were wearing. High fashion, rank – and piety – all came naturally together. For this was, of course, Suffolk society's last breath before the Reformation.

We find Edmund Blunden's grave. 'Poet', it says. When I put him on the London train after a talk he gave me his notes. His handwriting was a present in itself. He lies not many steps from the old mill house that Siegfried Sassoon bought for his retirement.

Trinity Sunday at Little Horkesley, with the oaken knight and his wives fast asleep, waiting for Judgement Day, and ourselves making our 'confession of a true faith to acknowledge the glory of the eternal Trinity, and in the power of the Divine Majesty to worship the Unity'. I say the collect carefully.

Movement, Stillness

A PEERLESS summer day. A little figure, sexless at this distance, whirls an ancient haymaker around on the slope. Its click-clatter joins that of my old typewriter. Once, a pair of youthful electricians paused in their work to tell each other, 'Listen, a typewriter!' Listen, I tell myself when the haymaking pauses, larks! And there they are, perhaps a couple out of sight but never beyond hearing.

The haymaker stacks bales in oblongs that deserve to be entered for the Turner Prize. Creamy florets of bloom cover the elder bushes, and the radio, should it slip over from music, speaks of billions. Always billions. There is trouble ahead, mark my words.

But it is summer in England; so walk in the present. The

great apostles Peter and Paul, and the wary Thomas, command the calendar. Some would have me pray for rain, but no fear! Oh, true hot June – do not dampen it. The white cat stretches under roses, talking in her sleep or possibly praising God. Who can tell?

To think that, as I speak, thousands are queuing at airports in search of the sun. It is here in the Stour Valley, heating up the willows, the water, Tom's herd of Lincolns, church towers, and silvery acres of onions, Neolithic flints, and gravestones.

Summer nights are still. After the Red Sea had drowned his pursuers, Moses saw his enemies 'as still as a stone'. This was one of the passages that Dame Diana Collins flinched from reading at Mount Bures. 'Oh, poor innocent horsemen; oh, dear horses!' But Miriam danced to the timbrel. And then they all walked on to Elim, with its 12 wells and 70 palm trees, and thus to the wilderness of Sin. Where they whined and complained. For such is human nature.

Diana and her husband, Canon John Collins, helped to lead black South Africans out of apartheid. I would see them at Mount Bures, but with no visible evidence of their greater role. Last Sunday, walking in the churchyard, I found the grave of their hedge-cutter, a mighty man with the shears. He lies alongside his mother, who died in the act of pouring him a cup of tea.

Stillness is always to be sought for. It is enchanting. The great prophet Elijah, pursued by the wicked Queen Jezebel, and terrified, hears God speak in a still, small voice after listening to him in thunderous expectation of his command.

These still words were Thomas Hardy's favourite in the whole of scripture, and they are engraved on his window in Stinsford Church. The New English Bible has: 'And after the fire, a low murmuring sound', which suggests to me that the modern translator had been reading E. M. Forster's *A Passage to India*. Caves boom, echo, distort, or tell unbearable truths. They are hollow, but not still.

At midnight, the Valley is tremulous with summer movement, and yet at the same time profoundly still. The mill pool, if you listen hard, will, now and then, faintly splash with rising fish. And sometimes a wind that you cannot hear will disturb the dragging leaves at the water's edge, or make the corn talk dryly or the sleeping birds settle more comfortably. A minute orchestra plays in order to create stillness. Nature's still, small voice precedes the fire of the dawn chorus, and is worth lying awake for. Elijah went to see his successor, and found him ploughing.

Lost Ships

A CREAMY bird-ridden dawn. Switch off the entirely horrible News. No balance there. The starving white cat bounces around on the scrubbed table. O pity, pity. Her green eyes glitter greedily. I think of George Herbert easing his poor young limbs from the damp sheets to find his way to the eastern window with his lute for his morning song. 'Lord, as I wake I turn to you, Yourself the first thought of my day.'

My eastern window reveals that I have accidentally

created a horticultural Paul Nash by white mullein near the ancient quern, which came from his Buckinghamshire garden, and by allowing Iceland poppies to soar all around. This year, the quern does duty as a bird restaurant, and is all a-flutter.

Stephen, who writes about naval archaeology, arrives, and complains that the cake is mouldy, and so it is, although it has been in the tin for less than a month. We talk about Whitby and drowned sailors. How they were never named. How they sailed away and sank in the anonymous depths. Mud would preserve their clothes. The penny in their pocket would go on shining, as would their bones.

His lost ships sail on the computer, fully manned, and sink there, too. Too many to calculate. Down, down, they went. Women went to the window every morning, time and time again, because nobody told them that they could not come home. Oh, poor Tom Bowling. Stephen and I eat Prince Charles's biscuits.

To the Oxfam shop to give a reading and do some book-signings. Familiar faces from Woodbridge. Yachts on the Deben. Boatsheds, tanned faces, smartened-up fishermen's pubs, plenty. But here and there the same windows where, long ago, the girls watched. Rolling Suffolk skies, glorious trees, football flags on cars, everything moving, waving as in a Dufy painting.

Back at Bottengoms, a June jungle-land where old roses are doing what they like, bursting over paths, reaching for the roof, drowning us in scent. Late News, extra-horrible. Poor Schumann's last songs on the other wave. They are about the final meditations of Mary, Queen of Scots, each brief and marvellous, and new to me.

Churchyard explosion on the answerphone. What did Stevie Smith say as she wandered around the graves? 'I love the dead, I cry, I love each happy, happy one.' At least they were beyond *The Churchyard Handbook*.

My favourite churchyard when I lived near Woodbridge was Boulge, where Edward FitzGerald lies under a rose from Omar Khayyám's tomb in Iran. I would cycle to it and lie in the tall grasses, listening to Mr Anderson's sheep blaring through the hedge and smelling the bull-daisies, and thinking of a short story.

'It is God that hath made us, and not we ourselves' had been carved on FitzGerald's stone, a line that would have done equally well for Omar. There were mown paths between summer thickets, illegible names, done-for dates. Lady White's husband. I would have tea with her. Thin, shallow cups, warm, fresh scones. A butler.

She was fragile, almost not present, her hands like skeletal autumn leaves that blow along the lanes. 'Where did you leave your bicycle?' She knew folk who knew Fitz. 'A very odd man. But then it wouldn't do if we were all alike!'

Paul Nash and Romney Marsh

A FLYING visit to see Kentish friends, the heatwave blown away here and there by Channel winds. Peering through the rooftops, I think I can see France. They take me to Romney Marsh, and we have a swift yet unhurried in-and-out tour of its Norman churches, St Mary in the Marsh, Ivychurch,

Bilsington, Bonnington, each perched on its tussock, all of them massively buttressed to prevent them sinking into the peat. Hefty and lovely, they rise against the falling sun.

The Marsh is as level as a board, other than where its dozen or so churches stand, and are sunken below the Weald. We discover E. Nesbit's grave with its bedhead memorial, something so tender, the work of her craftsman husband; and we remember Ken's

Teach me to live, that I may dread
The grave as little as my bed . . .

They wouldn't allow it now, bed-posts among the churchyard bull-daisies. Not far from the author of *The Railway Children*, a model railway continues to chug pupils to school.

The Marsh churches were all built by the Normans in the twelfth century, crowding the ground like the marsh sheep. The Normans found wood, and left stone, most of it rafted from Normandy. So, apart from its excellence, were they floating across the water the most enduring aspect of their native land? Then, soon, the subsidence and the buttresses. And now, the homely beauty, the trees dancing through the east windows, the interior treasures.

I heard a lot about Romney Marsh from my friend John Nash. His brother Paul had gone to live there immediately after they completed their official War Artist paintings in 1920. Paul found 2 Rose Cottages in Dymchurch. He wasn't well. Four years on and off the Western Front had left their mark, although it was not a bullet mark. Many soldiers suffered thus – still do, vide the non-wounded veterans of Iraq, with their sickness.

Paul Nash wrote: 'First sight of Dymchurch-under-the-Wall . . . New life in a different world . . . First paintings of Dymchurch Wall . . . Hard up . . . the Sea. The Shore. The Wall. The Marsh . . . T. E. Lawrence buys my first sea painting to hang in the Colonial Office to annoy the officials.' Paul would be back in Kent in the Second World War to paint the Battle of Britain.

On the way to my friend's house, we pass Spitfire Avenue, and I remember Paul Nash's marvellous aerial combats, the canvas exploding with starry fights, the vapour trails tangling in the sky, the brief smoke as a Heinkel (or a Spitfire) hits the Channel.

He described 'the river winding from the town and across parched country, down to the sea; beyond the shores of the Continent, above, the mounting cumulus concentrating at sunset after a hot brilliant day; across the spaces of sky, trails of aeroplanes, smoke tracks of dead or damaged machines falling, floating clouds, parachutes, balloons. Against the approaching twilight new formations of the Luftwaffe threatening.' No artist had painted such battles before.

At supper, there was talk of angels. How sensible of the medieval mind to provide God's messengers with wings, so that they could fly between earth and heaven. All over East Anglia, wooden angels roost above us, too high up for the Reformers' chopper.

Thomas Traherne

IT MUST end tonight, they decreed, the great heat; so I sat in the garden to watch it vanish in a thunderclap. The preliminaries were all that one could wish for. The sun went down in a sulky glory. The landscape went dark. The trees became monumental. The birds sang an octave lower. Two drops of rain fell on my head. Grunts and roars in an empty room betrayed Wimbledon running late. Pre-storm flower-scents filled the air. 'Break, break, break!' I quoted. But, in the contrary way in which weather works, it all blew over. No downpour, no lightning-rent skies, no finality.

Earlier in the day, some theology students from Cambridge came to talk about Thomas Traherne. How the voluminous quantity of his beautiful writings escaped bonfires and recognition for hundreds of years remains literature's puzzle. We spoke of his youth. So few years, so many pages.

I was with my Herefordshire friend Richard Birt at Credenhill long ago, the land of Traherne's *Centuries*. Although the amazing prose-poet threw out, as it were, a general invitation to his readers to find some Christian-cum-environmental bliss wherever they happened to be. Come rain or shine, given a chance, he would don a leather suit (like his Quaker contemporary, George Fox), lie under a tree, and stare through its leaves until his life's end.

Except that there was all this writing to do before one's mid-30s, when one would die. Would leave God's enchanting earth for heaven – an abstract which to him did not live up to the seasonal realities of Nature. For Traherne, angels were not up there but down here, playing in the streets when young, sitting in the sunshine when old. I don't doubt that if he came back to Hereford or Teddington at this moment, they would be there still; for our concepts of creation, when visionary, do not vanish.

Mercifully, today's ordinands do not have to seek influential sponsors in order to advance in the Church, unlike the youthful Traherne, who, in 1669, felt that the way up might be via Sir Orlando Bridgeman, Lord Keeper, an unquiet person.

How unlike the Bridgeman household was Susanna Hopton's circle at faraway Kington. Yet in and out of the Thames at Teddington, and in the London streets and squares, the always-young Traherne would have encountered those Christ-blessed bodies which he saw as a boy on the Welsh border, and which would not cease to entrance him.

The Church remained dubious of such joy. Every now and then, it broke out in curious writings and behaviour. But what could it do? The question is not obsolete.

As the weather decided not to break, I thought of Traherne in one of his rare moments of depression. 'At another time, in a lowering and sad evening, being alone in the field, when all things were dead and quiet, a certain want and horror fell upon me, beyond imagination . . . I was a weak and little child . . . Yet something also of hope and expectation comforted me from the border . . . This taught me that . . . the beauties of the earth when seen were made to entertain me.'

Earlier in the hot day, the Cambridge students talked of vocation and curacies, liturgy and sermons, of finding Traherne, and so many new things.

JULY

Suffolk Writers

EARLY MORNING in the heatwave, the air still and sullen, the trees cardboard shapes, the birds silent. One can almost hear the dead rose-petals falling. David's corn is a motionless bluey-green sea. At the moment, the day is holding back its potential and seems uncommitted, but in a little while the sun will spin up in the east like a gold coin. Yesterday, the washing dried in an hour.

The old house creaks a bit, and stays cool. Its pin-tiles cook. Strong eastern scents are burnt out of English roses. I watched a baby owl occupy one of those hedgerow elms that grow to 20 feet and then die. His baby feathers were as yet tumbled and unsettled. He looked down at me from on high. I mowed a bit, raked a bit, and heard a Wimbledon woman howling at every shot. I had left all the windows wide. The white cat, a Quietist, was sleeping the heatwave away under a bush.

On Friday, I went to the Aldeburgh Festival to talk about East Anglian writers. As usual, the North Sea was an immense wall about to fall on the borough. I met Martin Bell in the Jubilee Hall, and we sat on the stage, forsaking our notes, as we remembered his father, Adrian, the disturbing short-story writer Mary Mann, Henry Williamson, and the youthful Julian Tennyson, whose *Suffolk*

Scene lived in my bicycle basket throughout my teens.

Afterwards, Vicky and I called on Benjamin Britten, Peter Pears, and Imogen Holst in their graves at the far end of the vast churchyard, then drove home, running into the weekenders. Soon, for we each lived down old farm tracks, there would be only animals and children to greet us. And this heat. Late at night, I watered the tomatoes from the stream, and listened to a grown-up owl.

The Armed Forces Service was somewhat a surprise. A bugler arrived, and four British Legions. And George, a little boy, to read the familiar lines about not growing old. We sang Charles Wesley's 'Soldiers of Christ, arise' for the processional . . . 'Leave no unguarded place, no weakness of the soul.' And I draped the flags against a statue of St Alban, a British soldier in Roman uniform who had changed clothes with a priest so that he could escape death during the Diocletian purge of Christianity. Was Alban executed in vestments?

Anyway, my history sermon over, I returned the standards to their bearers, one as young as Alban, one as old as the Second World War, and we sang our way out into the sunshine. The Colonel had read the Beatitudes, which I had lengthened to include, 'Ye are the salt of the earth . . . the light of the world.'

When we ritually gather at the Crown for a pint, however, it is to find half-a-dozen of the congregation smoking outside in a kind of purpose-built veranda, and looking like boys behind the bike-shed. Inside the bar, we virtuous ones, including an Air Chief Marshal, politely discuss 'belief'. It is 28 June, the feast day of St Austol, who most likely gave his name to St Austell. An absolutely idle afternoon, barring a few weeds, then evensong without bugles. The grit from the new road repairs flies up like hot deterrents.

The Great Bindweed is out and climbing the sloe bushes in the track, trumpeting summer. Its huge white bells peal from the ditch. It was called Morning Glory in Somerset, and may have given its name to the even more glorious Ipomoeas of New England.

Valuable Men and Things of No Worth

IN DIOCESAN geography, I stand on the river-line between 'my' two cathedrals – St James's, at Bury St Edmunds, and St Mary the Virgin, St Peter, and St Cedd, at Chelmsford. Often, on Sunday mornings, as I announce the first hymn at our village matins, I hear their joint singing and see their familiar faces. How fine this equidistant worship is; not even Amos could object to its grandeur.

This Sunday at Wormingford it is 'Disposer supreme, and Judge of the earth', and a procession of two. The south door is open wide on to burnt grass, and bees haunt the warm stones. A score of mostly male voices do justice to a cathedral-size hymn.

It is the combined work of a seventeenth-century society poet and a nineteenth-century Tractarian. Jean-Baptiste de Santeuil was asked to make the countrified Paris hymn-book more fitting for the gentry to sing, and Isaac Williams, Keble's friend, and the translator of 'Disposer supreme', restored its holiness and its universality.

Williams became Newman's curate. They said that his relationship with him 'had long been a curious mixture of the most affectionate attachment and intimacy, with growing distrust and sense of divergence'. Williams wrote three of the *Tracts for the Times*. We score or so of 'frail earthen vessels, and things of no worth' rise to the occasion and sing – if I may say so – extraordinarily well.

The long, successive summer days are blissful. At the moment – it is 7 a.m. – birds are swinging on the mullein spikes like steeplejacks. All the windows are wide. The white cat lies upside down. The white horse rolls over and over. The newspapers sprawl unread. The early strangers on the farm track pause and point. What shall I do today? Nothing. On the radio the talk is, as ever, of billions. Thus it can be ignored, for who can understand billions?

On television, the young leaders take podium and plane steps two at a time, wear beautiful suits, and stern smiles. All will not be well, they say. But it will this July day, never fear. It is a day for the philosophy of Thomas Traherne, not that of the market. What few days he had, and my own so numerous, so profuse. He would by no means make even half a century. His old men in the Hereford streets would be wonders to him. For Traherne, it was sacrilege to live other than fully. He reminds us:

> That all we see is ours, and every one
> Possessor of the whole; that every man
> Is like a God Incarnate on the throne,
> Even like the first for whom the world began.

Traherne is the great antidote to billions, the language of

BP, and of the cutters. It is mostly double Dutch to most of us anyway. Vast figures are announced new every morning to our incomprehension. Faith deals in pence for the most part – except for the Quota, of course. Cathedrals charge, which they should not. To do so is faithless.

Village School

OUR VILLAGE school is about to shut its doors after 170 years. It is a strange event. Thirteen children. Glowing OFSTEDs. Glorious scenery. Reluctant parents. Victorian Gothic. I was a governor for ages, and an occasional storyteller. Cars bumped their way to it over the sleeping policemen. Head teachers came and went. Lovely new classrooms were built on a meadow. Now, silence and stillness, for ever and ever.

I am reminded of Laurie Lee's wild farewell to his village school in Gloucestershire, as he walked away with his fiddle and his future. Our school had its crowded past, but no tomorrow. Somebody will live in it and hear, if they are quiet, the farmworkers' boys and girls singing the assembly hymn. This would have been a long time ago.

Back once more from the John Clare Festival at Helpston. Our Society has outgrown the school named after him, and has to fill a marquee. Rows and rows of familiar faces. The village has wide Enclosure roads and handsome Barnack-stone houses, toppling hollyhocks, and bird-filled skies. As always, I see the poet running over the fields to Glinton, to be taught to read and write for a penny a week, and to do his arithmetic in the dust of the threshing barn, and to lie hidden with a book in a deserted quarry.

What a good education he got, one that was perfect for our greatest rural voice. Clare, too, had a violin. The gypsies showed him how to play it. We had lunch in the Blue Bell, where he would be found with his beer and his finds – wild-flowers. They would straggle from his velvet pockets. Have you read John Clare? If not, do so at once. His life was bitter-sweet with a vengeance. Poor Clare. Great Clare.

Visitors bump down my farm track, where there are no sleeping policemen: only ruts and rabbit holes, loppity verges, rises, and brief levels. But there are baby owls and whitethroats, cascades of July bindweed hanging from the sloes, where the parched wheat has recovered from a dry season.

Having mown all the grass, I sit outside, reading that curious book *The Cloud of Unknowing*, which I take to every now and then in order to feed my uncertainties. Its author, Richard Rolle, died in 1395, and, as he contemplates God in his short lifetime, he – as his editor, the wonderful Clifton Wolters, reminds us – explains what contemplation is.

That 'it is not the pleasant reaction to a celestial sunset, nor is it the perpetual twitter of heavenly birdsong. It is not even an emotion. It is the awareness of God, known and loved at the core of one's being. In this awareness there may be no overtone of beauty, nor indeed any sort of pleasurable response at all.'

While this may be so, I remain enchanted by Rolle's 'asides'; for, my goodness, how he can write! As I read him, I hear the cathedrals going up, and the faith with them. He knows that few are able to reach such heights, however, either in stone or belief. So he says: 'Not all those who read this book, or hear it read or spoken of, and as a result think it is a good and pleasant thing, are therefore called by God to engage in this work because of the pleasant sensation they get when they read it.'

He is a teacher who does not seek recruits. He certainly enjoyed the Middle Ages.

Second Helping

IT IS JULY 1827; so what would be happening? The bedroom is centuries older than this. It is about six o'clock, and, outside, the white cat lifts up her face piteously. She thinks she is passing away due to starvation. Three horses take turns to gulp water at the tank, and the oaks promise heat. All this could have been happening.

I check in John Clare's *The Shepherd's Calendar*, and am relieved to find that the shepherd is flat on his back reading a book, for our view of the past is one of incessant labour. But what work there is, is a romp, for the meadows 'are mad with noise Of laughing maids and shouting boys Making up the withering hay'. I stare down on the farmyard, now a sea of tall nettles, in whose depths lie the footings of pigsties, barns, and the stackyard itself. Not a murmur. Not a bird. Just a cat praying for a last bite.

Years ago, we lunched with friends who offered opposing amounts of food; one just enough, the other – like certain pubs — more than we could cope with. One said,

'Have you had your second potato?': the other urged, 'Do, please, help us out. It won't keep.' And would push third helpings in our direction.

After we left our first host, we always remarked, 'An elegant sufficiency', and laughed. When we said goodbye to the other host, we said nothing, being too full.

I thought of them as I heard on the radio that supermarkets dumped huge amounts of excellent food daily. Could there be anything more disgusting? Apparently, supermarkets have to be cornucopiac, pouring food from their shelves, else we would not be able to believe in their providence. They buy in sometimes a third more than they can sell – beautiful food – then throw it away.

In the post at least once a week come the starving Africans with their charity begging-bowls. It is a long time since they had their first potato. Will my unmissed five pounds help? It makes no more than a flutter when I measure it against the good, unsaleable food in the supermarket dustbins.

Is Alan Milburn our Barack Obama? I heard him this summer morning, lucid, smiling of course, fresh as a daisy, and this before the parliamentary recess. 'But,' said the interviewer, 'your government is on the way out . . .' She was clearly puzzled. But on he went, not noisy like the haymakers, but full of life.

I thought of 'sufficiency'. St John, it is thought, lived to be very old, and the young men plagued him about his memories of Christ. What was he like? What did he look like? What did his voice sound like? They longed to know.

But the ancient apostle's answer skated around these questions, and he would say: 'Little children, love one another.' That was all. And when they said: 'Is that all?' he would add, 'It will suffice.' If I had to moralize at this time it would be to urge sufficiency. Religiously, we should not ask for more. We have enough.

In July 1827, a farmer's family was making my old house rattle. The copper was bubbling. The bread oven was on the go. The washing hung on the bushes. The lovers laid in the corn. The cows cooled off in the pond. The vicar stood by a grave. Who slept in my room? Who hung his coat on that nail?

At Eventide

THE CONCLUSION of a Christian day. The still-fierce sun drains the light from the altar candles. They waver, pale and milky. The heavy presence of summer flowers. The giant oaken knight and his successive oaken wives raise imploring stumps. *Ora pro nobis*. The reformers lopped off their praying hands. Some 30 of us sing evensong: 'Lighten our darkness, we beseech thee, O Lord'.

The young priest who has been a prison chaplain all day is in the congregation. I should have said the prayer which asks God to pour upon him 'the continual dew of thy blessing'. But I say the evening prayer with which Robert Louis Stevenson ended the day in Samoa.

'Our guard is relieved, the service of the day is over, and the hour come to rest. We resign into thy hands our sleeping bodies, our cold hearths, and opened doors. Give us to awake with smiles . . . make bright this house of our habitation.'

Most days this week, I have sat outside this house of my habitation, listening to the late birds, pondering the reduction of a wild garden. For, as the Preacher did not say, there is a time for cutting beds and a time for the grassing-in of beds. But what a business it is. The deed is partly done, however, and I have the aches to prove it. Also, it looks surprisingly nice.

Which is why I am sitting where generations of farmers rested in July. Their hay was in, their corn stood high. And they ached and ached and ached, and it was somehow blissful to be seated in the fading light with a blackbird calling. To rest. It was warm, it would soon be dark. Just over the wall, the animals rustled themselves into sleeping positions; just over the hill, the flock faded from sight. It was Abrahamic.

I give myself a little drink, having no idea what a unit is. The white cat looks down from a column. St John's wort blazes away, having, it was said, been given a double dose of the sun. When, as I usually do, I used a sprig of it to lighten my Baptist sermon, the churchwarden told me that it was a weed, and what a bother it was to dig it out. The saint, said his bereaved Cousin, 'Was light – a burning and a shining light.'

Friends telephone, and trust that they are not disturbing me. Once, having to supply an address and gone to the study, I lose the phone itself until I hear it crying from a flower pot. 'What are you doing?' ask the friends. Nothing. I am seated at the entrance to my tent, waiting for angels to come over the hill.

'What? Are you all right? Did you watch Wimbledon?' How can one say on the phone that one is praying? It is so unreasonable. Or that one is wonderfully worn-out with gardening. George Herbert was wonderfully worn-out with music and words and God and just being alive, and with singing his evening window-hymn, because so much had to be compressed into so few years. Ditto Robert Louis Stevenson.

Theirs was the same fate, the consumption. The sickness which consumed you. Not long to sit by the door watching the sun sink into the glorious west. Yet long enough to achieve immortality.

On the radio, a woman who is almost 100 years old worries about her future and her possessions.

Blue

'BEAUTIFUL hymns,' says Barry appreciatively, as a score or so of them drift from matins. They will come and go all week as he trims the churchyard, as hymns do. His favourite hymn is St Bernard's 'Jesu, the very thought of thee', which its author described as 'Honey in the mouth, melody in the ear, a song of jubilee in the heart.'

St Bernard himself was beautiful, they said – brilliant, aristocratic, everything, but he chose to rule the world from a cell. His 'Jesu' was called 'the sweetest and most evangelical hymn of the Middle Ages'. It is younger than our tower.

That evening, I listen to Beethoven's late quartets overriding the cuts, and watch the barn vanish in the fading light. 'Jesu, our only joy be thou, As thou our prize wilt be.'

We encountered a badger in the track, bundling along, rolling out of sight in the bracken, crashing about.

Early next morning, I found the great field powder-blue from end to end. Flax, maybe, or blueness unequalled from lane to lane. Oil and fibre like a summer sky on the land, all spread out in a blueness unparalleled.

There were fields like this, and other pure hues like the oblongs in my paintbox, gloriously daubed on the countryside from Long Melford to Clare when I was a boy. Piecework girls picked flower-heads to make scent. It was always hot, and travellers set up gaudy fairgrounds on the green.

But the 59-acre flax field by the farmhouse has an intense blue silence, and is like blue glass in an ancient window, such as the one George Herbert told us to see heaven through. But is my flax linseed? Blueness is so mind-blowing. Flax for linen, linseed oil for printers' ink, blueness for paradise. The petals fall every afternoon, they say.

The most colourful words in the Bible are probably in the Book of Esther, when King Ahasuerus ordered his Queen, Vashti, to appear at his party, and she refused. Was she some pretty woman of his to be shown off to his friends? Was she not the Queen? It is an operatic moment. Her husband might rule 127 countries, but she was not his chattel.

And here comes the blue part. She was to come before his guests 'Where there were white, green, and blue hangings, fastened with cords of fine linen and purple to silver rings and pillars of marble: the beds were of gold and silver, upon a pavement of red, and blue, and white, and black marble.' But Vashti never came.

Unfortunately, King Ahasuerus was drunk, having been at the party a week, or he might not have done what he did. Which was to more or less divorce his wife in order to show that he was master in his own house. He told all his provincial governors to be masters in their own houses and not to stand women's tantrums. Which they did, according to the law of the Medes and Persians.

The wonderful Esther succeeded the proud Queen, a more intelligent lady, and used her position to promote her people, the Jews. I always hear trumpets blowing, and see that red, white, and blue pavement, when I read this exotic tale.

All the other 'blue' references in the Bible are to clothes. A modern poet who referred to 'Mary blue' used to enrage an old rector I knew. He would stamp up and down.

AUGUST

Maggie's Funeral

MAGGIE'S FUNERAL: the sun hot, the crowding cars burning. She was my most stately friend, tall, ancient, beautiful. She used to read for me when I took retreats. I read for her W. B. Yeats's 'The Wild Swans at Coole', and the poet's nine-and-fifty-swans, 'wheeling in great broken wings', bell-beat their way through the Perp aisles. Maggie herself had flown into Suffolk from New Zealand, but long ago.

Afterwards, in her garden. White wine and gossip, her August flowers nodding. They were building a new bridge over the River Box, and the sub-structure gleamed and the shallow water seemed hardly to deserve being called a river. But, as we all knew, come February, come floods. Come swans, too, 'Among what rushes will they build . . .?'

Pevsner, describing Boxford church, uses phrases such as 'exceedingly swagger', and 'pretty', and 'all rather wild', which makes one think of medieval joy. How often I cycled here when I was a boy, to hang over the rail and watch the roach and perch swim by. Now, I hear Maggie's dark voice, 'Yes, darling . . .'

The TV aerial has come adrift. Bits of it rock on the chimney, and the screen is a blank. There is such a thing as the luxury of deprivation. No more raucous Wark, but also, alas, no more of those delightful journeys with a camera. I rarely watch before 8 p.m., but then, if I am alone, a couple of hours of old film or new travel is no bad thing.

All the same, the fact that I haven't summoned the aerial man to mend the strange gadget that beams them in says something. Wood smoke billowed from this chimney when Shakespeare was writing *Twelfth Night*; so maybe it has shaken off the indignity of these wires. Some friends do not have television, and they appear quite well.

Stubble caught alight in the great heat, the flames running amok as in the bad old days, the horses whinnying, the straw crackling. An hour of this, with accompanying fear, then a kind of burnt-out silence. Then blackened acres and no harm done.

It is hard to imagine now that stubble-burning was a normal part of the farming year – a hellish aftermath of harvest. There were agriculturalists who sang its benefits, and who assured us that it was progress. Always doubt 'progress'. It is sometimes progressive to return to what was, to what was long-tested and found best. Yet, at the same time, we have to be visionary. Remember Lot's wife.

What does the white cat remember? What does she see ahead? The next meal omitted, of course. She stretches full length on the garden bench, eyes mere slits, tail listless. She could be listening to rooks. She stays out all night, and walks under stars.

I have picked the greengages. They fell lusciously into my palm, some sticky with juice, others with a skin bloom which it seems an outrage to touch. The deep freeze is filling up. Runner beans next. I have scythed the orchard with the lovely light scythe that Roger Deakin gave me, bringing down the seeding growth with mighty sweeps, and letting it lie. Strange to realize that it will be primroses next.

Cats and Walls

'AUGUST for the people,' said Auden. And the people for the A12. So stay at home, I said.

A little bit of woodland clearing grew into an ambitious amount of nettle-scything and sawing down of some already toppling crack willows (*Salix fragilis*); and by midday I was creating what never in my life had I thought of creating before, a glade. For I saw what the nettles etc. had hidden from me: a perfectly fitted carpet of ivy, and the pearly evidence of disturbed snowdrops.

Thus I toiled all day, virtuous and solitary. The overgrowth had long since hidden a farmyard wall that had kept the animals from straying into the orchard. The white cat, being addicted to walls, observed the emergence of this one with excitement, and, once it had been cleared and brushed down, walked its length rather showily; and, when the 'Suffolk whites' – the somewhat unsettled bricks – had been warmed up by the sun, stretched herself out for the day.

A few of the willows had obligingly fallen far enough for me to cut off their tops nice and tidily before tackling their trunks. By early afternoon, the glade appeared. I prayed that the August people would not do likewise, would not have what they called 'a run out to see' me, and break into my labour with their Bank Holiday. But they didn't; and by sundown I finished doing what at breakfast had never before crossed my mind. And now I wanted them to see what I had done, so that I could boast.

The following day, I went to Stowmarket to talk about John and Paul Nash and Carrington to the best small U3A group ever. Previous invitations had confronted me with halls full of members of such varying intelligence, if one is allowed to say this, that it became impossible to 'pitch' the address. Here, about 20 women and two men had met twice a month to study art, supplementing the talks and discussions with visits to galleries. It was beautifully manageable, and for the first time I began to recognize the value of this organization.

Stowmarket is one of those partly industrialized East Anglian towns that have always held a fascination for me. It was where my teenage father, plus countless boys from the farm, took their first steps to Gallipoli in 1914. Whenever the Norwich train stops at the station, I look out to see the exuberant throng, scared, thrilled, singing, innocent, by the same cast-iron platform pillars, their homely luggage in piles, their faces tanned from the fields; for it was August for the people.

Driving to the U3A talk, we slowed down to glimpse John Milton's mulberry tree. A visit to his Cambridge tutor, who was now Rector of Stowmarket, was commemorated with its planting. Mulberries and yews live for ever. Both say: 'I was there.'

God in the whizzing of a pleasant wind
Shall march upon the tops of mulberry trees,

declared George Peele, a poet Milton would have read but not have emulated. Mulberries should not fruit too near a house with pale carpets, else the floor will look like a recent murder. A single trodden fruit will produce an indelible stain. But the tree itself will last and last, seeing us all out.

Walkers, Wanderers, Vagrants . . .

A PALE but warm sun lightens the wet fields. The lawns are soggy and too rain-laden to cut, and the old roses look like old mops. But the runner beans are away. Tomorrow we are due to explore the hills and holes at Barnack, the open-cast quarry near Peterborough where the poet John Clare hid from prying village eyes to write. The weather forecasts are watery, but we'll go all the same.

Like those of all nineteenth-century – and earlier – folk, the accounts of his rambles usually mention the people he encountered, although they took second place to the birds and flowers. Stephen's do not. He is my best 'walking' friend. The descriptions of his walks are for me alone, although sometimes for his sister.

One has just arrived. It is beautiful, and as fresh as the hour when he started out – 4 a.m., at first driving a little way. 'Two things hit me as I got out of the car: the cold air, and a wall of birdsong, the last part of the dawn chorus.'

From then on, he takes me, his sole reader, into the lovely hidden Essex of 'the flat coastal plain towards Maldon, Bradwell, and the sea'. St Cedd's territory in fact.

But should Stephen pass another walker or worker, he will not mention him.

Nearly all foot-travellers of previous times say a great deal more about fellow walkers than they do about Nature – Nature in scientific terms, that is, although their descriptive handling of scenery can be superb. George Borrow (*Wild Wales*) actually walked so that he could run into characters for his books. And Francis Kilvert's *Diary* is an unconscious social history of the poor as they moved about: penniless lads, old soldiers, and vagrant workers, each of whom would catch his kind attention for an hour or so. Wordsworth made such briefly met tramps immortal.

Ancient laws were fierce about vagrancy, but, in summer, countless 'travellers' descended on our East Anglian fields to pick the peas, hops, and fruit. All have gone. No longer do the village pubs display chalked disgust – 'No Gypsies, no Irish, no Tramps'. Such essential labour was paid, but not thanked.

This vanishing of itinerants, this now complete absence of the seasonal strangers, has played havoc with the rural short story. Masters of this literary genre, one of the most difficult and among the most entrancing forms of fiction, are robbed of the dramatic disturbance caused by the stranger on the road.

Read A. E. Coppard, H. E. Bates, and many of the other great twentieth-century writers, and you will see how rich and strange – and dangerous – the market towns and villages were when the old lanes were being tramped down even further by a travelling mixture of workforce and idling force, as they had been for centuries. All gone; all disappeared over the hill.

The Sunday newspapers have a section on Walks. They give maps and mileage and historical information. Little is left to chance. But 'chance' should be the pearl of any walk. The chance for Stephen on his 4 a.m. walk was that the world would give him its 'early showing', and it did.

Walking to church, or to the village shop, I hope for nothing in particular, but not once have I reached the half-lost farmhouse without the award of some kind of tramp-prize.

Although it can never be of the curious quality that a 1930s walk, say, would almost certainly give, it will add something to the day. Someone I do not know has greeted me by my Christian name.

John Clare's Hills and Holes

A WILD DAY out at the Hills and Holes, the open-cast limestone quarry at Barnack (Northamptonshire) from which they hacked the medieval cathedrals and churches. It is an absurd adventure – Harry by fold-up bike, train, and hired car from London, Francie and myself by smoky car and fenland train from Wormingford.

Barnack is Monday-quiet. The Hills and Holes are a redeemed version of Paul Nash's shelled Western Front landscape. We hobble up and down its rucked floral carpet, silenced by the sheer extravagance of its August flowers and butterflies.

Here is the richest wasteland ever. Nature has drawn a colourful veil over the scars left by centuries of quarrymen.

Francie the botanist is so overwhelmed that she is often too delighted at what she sees to tell us what it is. Apart from one of those voluntary groups who lop and tidy these rare spots, and two maybe 14-year-old girls who have strayed out of *As You Like It*, and have built a perfect branch and grass house, no one else is about.

In my mind's eye, I see John Clare, the once haunter of the Hills and Holes. He is sprawling on his back on the furry limestone, one arm shading his face, the other flung across the flowers. The most wonderful of these is the Pasque Flower (*Anemone pulsatilla*) which blooms at Eastertide and is so beautiful that words can barely describe it. In eastern England they used to call it Danes' Blood.

John Clare belonged to a local archaeological group, and he once wrote to his London publisher:

25 March 1825

You have often wished for a blue Anemonie . . . and I can now send you some . . . I could almost fancy that [it] sprang from the blood or dust of the romans for it haunts the roman bank in this neighbourhood & is found no where else . . . [it] did grow in great plenty but the plough that destroyer of wild flowers has rooted it out of its long inherited dwelling.

No plough would ever have ventured on to the Hills and Holes of Barnack. Once the quarrymen had departed, their sharp territory vanished beneath a thin covering of lime-soil in which, like the young poet, the ancient flora of eastern England could find refuge.

It was breathtaking. We trod ridges and dells and were entranced. Then we found the quarrymen's pale church. I imagined them white and dusty at mass, one eye on the priest, the other sizing up an arch, and singing a lost hymn.

I took Francie and Harry to Clare's grave, so familiar to me, so new to them. And then we made our eccentric ways home by folding bike, hired car, smoky car, and a train.

Peterborough and Ely cathedrals shone through the carriage windows. Crops hid the black earth, but nothing hid the flatness. Whittlesea, whose 'sea' has dried up; St Edmundsbury with its new tower lending significance to a low roofscape; and then, weary like children after an adventure, down the flint track home.

August of the henbane (*Hyoscyamus niger*), a charming Hills and Holes plant full of poison. Easter for the Pasque Flower filled with blood.

The Dream and Dragonflies

I HAVE BEEN re-reading John Henry Newman. What a peerless writer. It is his prose and poetry that qualify him for sainthood. He wrote his own epitaph – *Ex umbris et imaginibus in veritatem* – 'From shadows and symbols into the truth'. Thus he joins St Paul and his dark glass, and the author of *The Cloud of Unknowing*. He was in his early sixties when he wrote *The Dream of Gerontius*, maybe thinking that he could not go on much longer. But he went into the bright darkness at nearly 90.

Just imagine going to church and hearing the young clergyman in the pulpit preaching: 'O Lord, support us all the day long, until the shadows lengthen and the evening comes, and the busy world is hushed, and the fever of life is over, and our work is done. Then, Lord, in thy mercy, grant us a safe lodging, a holy rest, and peace at the last.'

In *The Dream*, Gerontius is told that it is his 'very energy of thought' which kept him going, as we would say, when he longed to be with God. In our petitionary prayers, I have taken to including those whose energy of thought has vanished, and who lie in the Alzheimer's corridors of the care home. Theirs is a very different cloud of unknowing. 'Who are you?' they say to their sons. Newman said that 'the world is content with setting right the surface of things'; so keep a lively eye on politicians.

Up the road, in Colchester, the Officers' Club has burnt down. Whoosh! All gone. It stood on a fascinating site in this Roman-Saxon town, and the archaeologists are wringing their hands in public and sharpening their spades in private. What a loss: what luck!

I think of the sprung dance-floor, the regimental silver, the laughter, the drink, the slender subalterns in their mess kit dancing to 'Roses of Picardy' or 'Begin the beguine', according to which war one happened to be fighting. And, between the wars, the crinkly old memsahibs from the Raj doling out bridge cards. And now all gone, all gone. Actually, the regimental balls and dinners took place over the graves of Benedictine monks. Not that their bones would have minded, I sense, their souls singing to another music.

Neighbours on the high ground talk of drought and burnt grass. Those of us who live in the hollows stay wet and green. Also, my dragonflies have taken off from the horse-ponds, as they do each August. These darting jewels fly low. *The Dragonflies of Essex*, which my friend Ted Benton gave me, is kept handy. Dragonflies breed in both moving-water and still-water sites, and are all over the place at Bottengoms Farm.

Ted's description of dragonfly weddings may not do for the *Church Times*, although a sample of his naturalist writing must be read. One form of dragonfly mating, he says, is like an illustration from the *Kama Sutra*, and 'is generally known as the wheel position . . . They may remain in the wheel position for a few minutes or up to half an hour, depending on species. If disturbed, they usually remain coupled and fly off to find an alternative hiding place.'

They are creatures of water, land, and air, and gorgeous to behold, darting and chasing, settling and vanishing. And not unlike us.

Sporting Cousins

'I CALL this a wet day without rain,' David says. He is on a high. The Community Orchard, on which he has set his heart and laboured for so long, is about to be planted. To crown it, he has discovered a hitherto forgotten local apple called 'Twining' after a curate, and he a member of the tea family. Our other local apple is the D'arcy Spice, of course.

Both will go into the Community Orchard this winter.

And, if this isn't excitement enough, David has found a rare spider in the wetland of the local Woodland Trust, of which I am patron. I swell with importance. The spider is called after a wasp because of its yellow stripes. Overcome with all this news, we have some sherry.

My cousins arrive from what was Huntingdonshire, and our talk is all of deaths and entrances, glorious weddings, and of how to give up fox-hunting without denying the thrill of the chase. We agree that no one anywhere should any longer amuse themselves by terrifying or killing animals. We applaud the new anti-bullfighting laws now being laid down in parts of Spain.

We remember our cousin Peter the cricketer, a beautiful man grown old and now gone, and how each of us slip away. Our cousin Winnie Blythe played tennis for Suffolk, and she has slipped away. There was a pile of Slazenger balls by the altar at her funeral. I worried in case they would topple when the organ went into top gear.

At matins, both lessons are incomprehensible – unless you have read fore and aft. Which, alas, few do. It is not that people should do Bible study, but just read for pleasure's sake. I have been reading William Tyndale's New Testament, and often can hardly put it down. This is the modern-spelling version by David Daniell, with its fascinating introduction. Why read Dan Brown tosh when one has this astonishing book?

Tyndale writes a prologue to each of the epistles. They are succinct and riveting. The one to Timothy is all about the behaviour of bishops. They should 'avoid vain questionings and superfluous disputings which gender strife and quencheth truth'. Tyndale sees Paul's Letters 'fighting for truth'.

The truth is all that Tyndale asks, and it was for this that the bishops of his day burnt his book and got him strangled, as it was so dangerous. What a wonderful Gloucestershire man he was. How one loves him as one reads on. How English he is. But how am I to get the lesson-readers to read on? Or back, if it comes to that?

It is chilly for mid-August. But the plums are fat, and the harvest goes on being cut between little rains. And the lawns are spring-shaggy, being too damp to mow. And, were it not too shocking a thing to divulge, I would tell how I switched on a bar or two when friends call, the old house maintaining its cool.

I plant poppy seed and collect sweet-pea seed from Italy, that is from the heavily scented plants brought here from Tuscany, something I do every year. The hollyhocks topple like sunstruck guardsmen, and wrens are everywhere. All we need are a few more degrees.

I listen to Henry James's *The Wings of the Dove* on the radio, which is about love and money. Had James been reading Jane Austen – 'It is wrong to marry for money, but foolish to marry without it'?

Southwold and Bunhill Fields

ARTISTS, wasps, and hornets murmur in the garden. The artists are painting watercolours and are strewn among the late summer flowers. One of them, Tim, comes in to announce that the greengages are ready. Oh my goodness! Not a minute must be wasted. Another couple of days, and the hornets and wasps will be at them. Firm, settling to squishy, they are delectable beyond words. A great many can be picked at arm's length, the high ones shaken down into the freshly scythed grass, disturbing the sleeping white cat, who loves a bit of hay. Soon they will be in the deep-freeze and in me.

A trip to Southwold in chilly sunshine. What a pretty place it is, all brick-red and casement-white. Cannons point out to sea to save England from the Dutch; the pier is for sale – only £6 million, nearly the price of a beach hut; and morris men dance on the sands. Music contests the crashing shore. The North Sea is profound ultramarine streaked with green. Nobody swims in it, other than Ian, that is, who declares it gorgeous.

We visit the Sailors' Rest and stare into the open faces of Victorian seamen. Drowned boys, burly old chaps in heavy jerseys, gaunt women. I would not have minded lolling in one of its comfy chairs all afternoon, smelling the past and its victories. Southwold is crowded, yet quiet; busy, yet still. The hard labour of yesterday is partly absorbed into the leisure of the present. George Orwell lived uncomfortably here in the 1930s. It could hardly be his scene.

There is a glorious church for St Edmund, all black and brilliant with flint, and the River Blyth estuary, the gulls wailing over it. We have tea by a hot cobblestone wall, and I think of day trips when I was a child, and the unbearable moment when we had to pack up the picnic and leave the seaside.

At matins, I celebrate John Bunyan's Day. Poor, massive

old saint: news had come to him of a rift in a London congregation between father and son; so he set off on his horse to knock heads together. It was a long way from Bedford. Also it rained, even on the Celestial Mountains (the Chilterns); so he got soaked, caught a chill, and died. They buried him in Bunhill Fields.

This graveyard of the Dissenters was only three years old then, but soon Bunyan would be surrounded by William Blake, Isaac Watts, and Susannah Wesley, mother of John and Charles. How sacred this place. How Christ-filled these lives. How active still.

I once walked through *The Pilgrim's Progress* using a map made by Vera Brittain, Shirley Williams's mother, and saw everything in that divine book, from the Slough of Despond to the House Beautiful and the House of the Interpreter, from the Cross (at Stevington) where Christian shed his load (the author's anvil) to where the trumpets sound for him on the other side (of the Great Ouse). Britain's landscape provided that of salvation and paradise for our ancestors. Naturalists make sure that it does so still.

Duncan is tidying up the fields opposite. There is humming and crunching and gallopings as his horses make themselves scarce.

An Apostle for August

'AUGUST for the people and their favourite islands,' Auden wrote in August 1935, and, all these years hence, they, or we, continue to seek the same 'complicated apparatus of amusement'. Thus our branch of the Royal British Legion reinstates the Flower Show and the Fête. It rains, of course – warm, soft rain that makes the bouncy castle run like orange blancmange and the cake stall cover up.

'How wonderful', I say in my opening speech, 'that, although our post office and school have been taken from us, Jim and his friends have continued to provide these old August treats.' Underclad and damp, we trample the wet grass, smile at the soaking dogs, and look up at the sky and say: 'It won't be much.'

Politicians hurry back from beaches, apparently unaware of history; for August is not only for the people, but crises. Part-tanned, they make speeches in the road. The newspapers fret. But the people proclaim the spirit of 1935, and brave the seaside as if they still must make the most of a week's leisure.

In church, I preach on St Bartholomew, the August apostle, about whom we know virtually nothing. Even his name adds to his obscurity; for it tells us that he is the son of Tolmai, no more. Added to which it cannot be spoken without reminding us of an appalling massacre.

If any good can come out of such evil, we hereabouts did have our economy brightened by the arrival of the Huguenots when they fled from France. They were the Protestants who escaped from Catherine de Medici's bloodbath, and from countless later persecutions, to found our silk trade and another aristocracy.

But what made us dedicate the glorious church of St Bartholomew, in West Smithfield, to Bartholomew, ages before this Christian crime? Peter Ackroyd says that pilgrims to London in the twelfth century, when it already had the reputation of being a sacred city, prostrated themselves in this meadow, saying that a temple would be built on it 'which shall reach from the rising of the sun to the going down thereof'.

The founder of this church was Rahere, a man who made himself a fool for God. He was in Italy when he had a vision of St Bartholomew, who said: 'I, by the will and command of the High Trinity, and with the common favour and counsel of the court of heaven, have chosen a spot in the suburb of London called Smithfield, on which you are to build a tabernacle of the Lamb.'

Returning to London, Rahere called up an army of children, women – anybody – and told them to collect stones. Henry I gave him entitlement to the site, and so – St Bartholomew the Great, whose hospital became Bart's. 'Its narrative of construction', Peter Ackroyd writes, 'is a true representation of the fact that St Bartholomew's was a collective work and vision of the city; it became, in literal form, its microcosm.'

The shape of Tolmai's face is now identifiable. All around his church, for centuries, the people kept August holiday at what they called Bartholomew Fair. At matins, I read the collect: 'Grant, we beseech thee, unto thy Church, to love that Word which [Bartholomew] believed, and both to preach and receive the same.'

Later in the showery week, a neighbour who was descended from Huguenots and I drove to the coast where, in the brilliant light, holidaymakers splashed at the edge of the sea, holidaymaking dogs greeted each other, brave Englishmen took off their shirts, pennants whipped, and tea was served. August.

SEPTEMBER

Stoke Charity and Jane Austen

THE FIRST day of autumn, and very still. Matt-white cyclamen and crocuses in the summer mulch. Pale gold sky. It is six o'clock in the morning, and not a sound. I walk round the cool garden. Not a bird.

Someone close to me is likely to leave the world at this moment. Old and very ill, he will die. Will go to God. What happiness. Jane Austen died with her head on her sister's lap. She was 41. What a loss. Although perhaps not; for what more could she have done?

Thomas Ken advised the Winchester schoolboys to fear their graves as little as their beds. How unreasonable. I say prayers for all those who will leave this life today. September gathers pace outside.

Christine has been showing me Hampshire, steering me through the tall trees, pointing out the shallow rivers where the current barely covers the trout-fisher's boots. And here, suddenly, is Chawton, and we are trying not to tramp through the fragile house, although determined to see everything.

Ourselves, and a lot of other equally determined visitors, some of whose accents betray great journeys. We creak into the still-private rooms of these ladies, the two Cassandras and Jane, and are humbled by the simplicity of their possessions. The tiny scalloped table on which the immortal novels were written gives pause. Holds me up. Still somehow goes on breaking into my thoughts, now that I am back here at Bottengoms, where the Stour Valley air is different.

Besides Jane Austen, there was Stoke Charity Church, in which the holiness of the Middle Ages remains undisturbed. It is a field church standing close to watercress beds, and is wonderfully beautiful.

Trevor Beeson stood in the pulpit and wittily described its usually absent rectors. How could they bear to be anywhere else? Treasure after treasure; a carving of the mass of St Gregory, a lime statue of St Michael the Victorious, a miscellany of extraordinary objects like long-mislaid things in an old jewel box catch the eye.

But something very different caught the eye of the Revd William Buckland, a Victorian pre-Darwinist scientist – something that made pre-Reformation carvings look like recent toys, the fossilized existence of previous things. His science excluded. Buckland was certainly a very odd man, although no parson was too odd to be included on the average Incumbents' Board. Their tenures are marked; their voices are forgotten.

And now we have yet one more harvest festival. Or three, to be exact, as Wormingford, Little Horkesley, and Mount Bures at this time of the year, like every other parish in this country, go through the rite of pretending that they eat or starve according to the prosperity of their own fields, while doing their best to adapt their Harvest Homes to the terrible non-harvests of southern Africa and elsewhere. Or to such matters as the cuts promised by politicians and the gospel of Robert Peston.

So the fruit and veg will be piled up, and a real sheaf will appear in church. And I will go on reminding someone that a real loaf must appear on the altar. And we will sing the tragic hymn in which the angel of death reaps us; for it is sad to leave our fields, so newly ploughed and drilled for next year. To regret that we must die is a mark of gratitude for the earth.

Braes of Rannoch Church of Scotland

SCOTLAND is never England, even by a Border mile. If one had to sense the fleeting breath of some other culture, it would be that of France.

Scotland, which, when one is back home, looks like the tail-end of Britain, acquires a grand mileage when one is there, making it a very big place indeed. Range after range of mountains, endless lochs, countless glens, mystifying roads, and, where I am in Perthshire, vastly spaced-out houses that provide an intimate neighbourliness that is often closer than that of a Home Counties street.

I first went to Scotland in my twenties, clasping James Boswell's *Journal of a Tour to the Hebrides*, in which the young author hoped to dispel in his companion's mind the conviction that his native land was barbarous. Dr Johnson, his poor old body rolling along, had to admit that the noblest prospect that a Scotsman saw was not the high road that led to England. Persuading the great man to leave London for Skye was proof of the Doctor's love for his friend, not of his changed opinions where Scotland was concerned.

I carried this glorious travel-book on trains, buses, and on foot, tramping its map, now and then stumbling beneath its verbal blows as English literature's mightiest odd couple steered me hither and thither. All this a long time ago.

But now Christopher drives me to all the destinations made somehow sacred to us both by previous visits, and there they are: grim Ben Lawers, enchanting Glen Lyon, immense Rannoch Moor, mythical Fortingall (and also true Fortingall), and the first autumn leaves – silver birch – racing ahead of the car. Venison, haggis, and a nip of the malt on the table, and a hint of Kirk austerity as we push open, here and there, a solemn door.

The parishes are few and far between. Fortingall itself is more like a diocese in width and influence, its Celtic Christianity keeping its Presbyterianism informed. It is possible that the voice of St Adamnan is heard above the torrents still. Anyway, I can hear it – but then you know how fanciful writers' ears are, and not always to be trusted.

Each morning, the Highlands rearranges itself to create watercolour views. 'Look!' we cry. 'Did you ever see anything like it?' Yes, but only in Scotland. Each night, the harvest moon and Venus observe their images in the loch, and the sheep stop nibbling. But the Tay runs glitteringly every minute.

Each teatime we close the high deer-gate. In bed, a tremendous quietness rules us. I find myself remembering my Scottish neighbour in Suffolk, Mr Anderson, who was judge at the sheep fairs, and who looked out at our tableland mournfully though uncomplainingly. Were he not in heaven, I would send him a postcard.

The parish magazine lies on the chair. 'Braes of Rannoch

Church of Scotland linked with Foss and Rannoch Church of Scotland. Minister: the Reverend Christine A. Y. Ritchie, B.D., The Manse, Kinloch Rannoch, by Pitlochry, Perthshire . . .' The magazine is economically informed and impressive, with articles on the cuts, 'A Chill Wind', and the tourist management of a huge, lovely, empty area.

On the far side of 'our' loch there is the smudge of the Black Wood, a sliver of the prehistoric Caledonian Forest, where I once walked, looking for the red squirrel. It makes Adamnan seem quite recent.

At Rannoch

WHEN JOHN NASH left Bottengoms Farm for the painting holiday in Scotland, the Triumph Herald groaning with gear, easels, fishing rods, weighty clothes, and Penguin whodunits, there would be a tragic pause before he and his wife bumped up the track. He would take farewell of his garden. 'Only two weeks,' he would assure it.

Off to Scotland myself, I have mowed all the grass, trimmed the summer stragglers, done a good job on the more importunate overtakers of order, and packed my single case. I am a light traveller on trains. Also a devoted one, especially if they go a long way. The ride to Pitlochry will be blissful. Also holy, for the Northumbrian coast will slide past, and St Cuthbert's watery paradise will briefly fill my vision.

What a treat to be at Leargan again, the big white house above Loch Rannoch. Children like returning to the same holiday place, and so do I. We, the Scottish holiday friends and myself, will call on the mountains and glens we have come to know over the years. Maybe the pine marten will appear on the terrace wall, rushing us to the window.

A Victorian natural history says: 'The first in the list of Weasels are the agile and lively Martens, or Marten Cats. Pine and Beech – the difference between the two is mainly in the colour of the throat. Beech is white, Pine is yellow, and its brown fur is nearly as good as sable. The skins killed in the winter were worth 2/6, good money in those days.'

Our pine marten is grand and aristocratic, like the Scottish nobility in their stone castles; it is the rarest of our eight native carnivores, and is now more or less confined to the Highlands. The best way to look at them is to put some honey on a woodland tree and hide near in the early evening.

Scotland smells wild, or at least it does in Perthshire, on wild and fearful Rannoch Moor, and ditto Ben Lawers, and enchanting Schiehallion, the Fuji of Tayside, which seems to rise in every direction. Time was when we might have climbed to its tip, but now we are watchers, which is quite a good thing to be. Ye watchers and ye holy ones.

In Scotland, I can scarcely watch enough. Enormous landscapes fill my eyes, an emptiness that is also a fullness makes me look and look. Christopher, my host, has been seeing all this all his life, and will have been changed by it. Just as I have been moulded by East Anglia, I suppose.

The Scottish holiday is to me a kind of annual landscape meal where more than I can possibly devour is provided. We have been here in June and in September. In June, the wild flowers of the glens and marshy borders and tracks of the lochs are simply amazing. In September, the heather creates a kind of sadness or thoughtfulness which pervades the Scottish Psalter.

The Pope leaves as I arrive. Perhaps that quiet old man should have put on a warm jersey and tramped over Rannoch Moor for a day or two, and got its wind into his nostrils. Climate makes faith – or defines it. Vast churches exclude climate – those temples made with hands over which the Lord seemed to despair and mourn.

'*Very little White Satin . . .*'

'NEWS FROM a foreign country came,' wrote Thomas Traherne, memorably. It was about 'the unknown God'. Falling asleep between 'Book at Bedtime' and the shipping forecast, I miss the mostly bad news scrupulously gathered for me all through the summer's night. Dud elections, crime, flood, Andy Murray whacked by a Croat, bombs, etc. It was ever thus.

I take down the 1758–80 volume of *The Annual Register* and read: 'John Wilkes has surrendered himself to the king's bench prison'; that there are arguments for nursing the infant poor in the country; that Captain Dalrymple has a plan for providing distant countries with the conveniences of life; that a great many lords and ladies are dead; that Ireland riots; that the English are fighting the Indians at Detroit, and so on. News.

In Barclays Bank, two huge news-screens make sure that I do not miss a thing as I cash a modest cheque. What a seemly gentleman the Prime Minister is – not like that Signor Berlusconi. Their faces are not to be missed. The cashiers smile. The Arctic melts.

I read the last pages of *Emma* at the village wedding. Miss Woodhouse marries Mr Knightley. 'The wedding was very much like other weddings, where the parties have no taste for finery or parade . . . and where the predictions of the small band of true friends who witnessed the ceremony, were fully answered in the perfect happiness of the union.'

A quite large band of true friends, to be accurate. The neighbouring church was almost impossibly beautiful, the young priest devout and moving, the sun incredibly hot, the true friends no longer young, but wise, the singing grand, and the arrangements a credit to us all.

Afterwards, I searched about in the churchyard for Natalie's grave, and remembered her parties in the fine house where the peacocks strutted along the terrace and she was eternally lovely. 'It was her profile,' they said. Did I remember Natalie's profile? I remembered her 'Let's have a party' voice.

The September heatwave burned the tombs. All round the church porch, thousands of white rose-petals mixed with the scorched leaves. Women succeeded in kissing each other below vast hats; men sweltered in suits. 'Very little white satin, very few lace veils: a most pitiful business! Selina would stare when she heard of it' – Mrs Elton. And only one ring. But such rightness, such a country match. It could not have been bettered.

The big willow has fallen at last. For weeks it has lurched drunkenly across the old stackyard, swaying, grunting, sadly waving, blocking the view. And then, when the News was being wasted in my sleeping ears, it fell. Gave up. There it lies, all arms and legs, its last leaves fading, waiting for Paul and his chainsaw. In death, it filters the valley scene.

In his poem, Traherne says:

My Soul stood at that gate
To recreate
Itself with bliss, and to
Be pleased with speed. A fuller view
It fain would take . . .

There's a lot to be said for recreating oneself with bliss.

Mending the House

THE AUTUMN crocuses are out. Naked ladies. They stand in immaculate clusters here and there, but where I do not recall seeing them before, flowers of the utmost purity. And the ash leaves are flying, and geese, too. Will anyone remember if I preach last year's harvest-festival sermon? Since it was so good, I mean. And when will the rain stop?

It blows thinly through the garden, and Keith, who is replacing the Second World War soft-wood windows with hardier stuff, has to work from the inside. Scotland seems a world away. The afternoon sun will be splintering Glen Lyon; the surface of Loch Rannoch will be gunmetal grey.

I am trundling off to bookshops to sign copies of my new book, *Aftermath*, alongside Peter the publisher. How did book launches go in the thirties, say? Were there such things? I know that you were not a 'popular novelist' until you were chauffeur-driven, or retained a suite at the Ritz. Things have come to a pretty pass – one that the Government will applaud.

I make some tea for Keith and myself. I have watched artists paint, but rarely with the admiration I have for Keith as he saws and glazes, sizes and fits. In the spring, his window will fly open, and birds will take over its creamy sill. People will look out of it long after my sight has gone.

He has filled in all the cracks in the wall, and he will crown his labours with a new brass door-knocker. 'It must be ten years since I last done your house,' he tells me. Must it? Oh, golly! (I have been reading a post-war novel.)

I put out some five hornets per morning, including one from my hair. But mostly the beautiful creatures beat against a sash window in the guest room, where one should have been able to boast about them as a gift, though apparently not. Releasing them from the glass, they zoom off like Spitfires, all go. Soon, the frosts will make them take cover, and the old room will not hear their organ music.

I make sharp fruit salad with green grapes, the final plums, some miscellaneous apples, and some wrinkled mandarins. Waste not, want not. Spare me your economies, says the white cat, tasting my bare feet. No, I reprimand myself, at the benefice harvest service it shall be the story of Ruth and her return to Bethlehem, the house of bread, none other. The ancestors of Jesus were wed from its cornfield.

We shall send our produce to St Saviour's, Hoxton, where those holy women will turn it into soup and I don't know what for poor lads on the streets. What is harder and harder to get across to modern congregations is that harvest festival is not about charity but gratitude for what grows, what flows, what climaxes in the autumn. While the earth remaineth, seedtime and harvest shall never cease. So, say 'Thank you.' The newly authorized Druids have something to tell us on this point. So grateful was Egypt for the Nile harvest that the divine Pharaoh himself helped to cut it and bring it in.

We are to read Nehemiah, one of my favourites. It is he who inspired the rebuilding of Jerusalem, and the re-establishment of its government, and the purification of its customs. Its ruined towers stood up in the sand like autumn crocuses once more, and there was singing in the Temple.

The Little Horkesley Farm Walk

PEGGY and Roy come to lunch. Walking through the orchard, as they must, she sees the Victorian plums nid-noddering on the bough, pulling it to the grass. 'They aren't quite ready,' I tell her, meanly. She says that when she went to the fruit farm to buy 'half a stone', the man told her: 'They're a pound a pound, Peggy.'

'A pound of plums a pound?'

'That's what they are paying, Peggy.'

She picked plums on this farm during the war for a shilling a cart-load, let us say. I relent, and pick her a pound. She is a great gardener, and will notice the hulms of my devoured runner-beans straggling still by the door, and that the tomatoes are blighted. But late roses do me proud.

Roy, who knows more about churches and parish life in East Anglia than anyone else, talks about the Churches Conservation Trust, which is handy, as I have just visited St Mary's Old Church at West Bergholt. It has a beautiful 'arrested' feeling of being untouched by any of the late-twentieth-century changes. Airy and sacred, rather scrubbed-looking, and with rows of hat-pegs here and there, and a Saxon north wall doing sturdy service still, it breathed afresh.

I could have sat there for hours, but we – about 30 of us – were on the annual Farm Walk on a Sunday afternoon. A lane without a destination – well, a sugar-beet field – allowed us to divert to the wood from which the village probably derived its name. Coppiced ash and oak reached for the sky, and weedy green ponds watered the brambles.

The children, released from their computer dens (I am probably doing them an injustice), swarmed up trees, and the congregation, dressed for the part, shed decades. Then tea and open-air evensong, where I preached on 'Walk while you have the light', and a donkey from over the fence accompanied our hymns. And all the time the curiously affecting atmosphere of the Conservation Trust's church up the road hung around me, as it were.

There, at the west end, was the gallery where the farm labourers sang Merbecke to fiddles. There, in the impossibly ancient bell-turret, dangled a Victorian bell, its clapper dully visible, its cage nicely slapdashed with whitewash. And, strangely, over the chancel arch, were the arms of James I, only partly peeled away like one of those transfers we stuck on the back of our hands when we were boys.

Although under the arms was not the royal motto, but the first line of glorious Psalm 68 in Latin, maybe as a compliment to the king's famous learning. *Exurgat Deus Dissipenter Inimici* – 'Let God arise and let his enemies be scattered.' And it ends, 'O God, wonderful art thou in thy holy places.'

Why are not the West Bergholtians in this holy place? Because, in 1904, as it had become remote from the heart of the village, everyone saved up to commission Sir Arthur Blomfield and Sons, the firm that employed Thomas Hardy, to build St Mary (New) in their midst. Thus releasing St Mary (Old) to dwell in immense silence after near-on 1000 years of parochial clamour.

Hang your sun-hat on a peg and sit there. Read Psalm 68, in which 'thousands of angels' take a holiday from Sinai, and singers and minstrels, and damsels with timbrels, and 'little Benjamin', and the princes of Zabulon, and goodness knows who else kindly deputize for a vanished Essex choir.

Traherne's Happiness

TO DISCOED – 'the edge of the wood' – once more. This time to join in the re-dedication of a Bemerton-size church named, like so many of the shrines of the Marches, after Michael. Golden-grey October weather, the Radnor hills folding and unfolding ahead, the brief rains like curtains across the sun.

A decade or so ago, the poet Edward Storey came here to find this church over the garden wall. Though not decrepit, it had the worn face of a building that needed more than the annual spring clean. Its history was patchy and indistinct. Poor shepherd folk had kept it going, and I loved them for it.

The roundel in which a glass Good Shepherd had clasped a lamb was blocked. But, unusually, Joseph of Arimathaea, dressed boldly in his Grand Council robes – no skulking to his Lord by night – stood before the cross in the east window.

Since I last arrived, the whitewash of ages had been brushed away to reveal fine stonework, and the very rafters seemed to sing in their freshness. Outside, a yew vying with Time itself, like the one at Fortingall in Perthshire, trees that were old before Christianity, darkened the nave wall.

We sang angelic hymns, and I preached on 'The Temple'. Before this, I gave a talk on George Borrow and the Gypsies, and, of course, his *Wild Wales*, and Edward Storey read his wonderful Discoed opus. It was a great do. Writers frequently have these little pockets of faraway 'belonging', places where they put down a root or two, and where they have become guests. Stephen, the Rector, smiled.

And, of course, the annual walk around Presteigne; the annual rummage in the bookshops; the yearly look at the *Entry into Jerusalem* in St Andrew's, a sumptuous Tudor tapestry; and the yearly dinner with David and Simon at Bryansground, that perfect garden where I have planted trees, thus in a way extending my growing self.

And autumn visits to Stockenny Farm, with its faint smudge that is the Malvern Hills, and to Lower Rowley, where I half expect to see Samuel Palmer sketching. Then back to Bottengoms and to the white cat shaking her head, she who finds all she needs in my two acres and who tells me frankly that she has never heard of Liverpool Street, let alone Wales. Have not Alan and Pam fed her, doted on her? Would she have me believe that I have abandoned her? Yes.

On the way home, we drove through Credenhill, and I remembered Thomas Traherne. I imagined him having more happiness than was manageable, so that it had to spill over that Victorian book-barrow into my life – into everyone's life, eventually. And this during the terrible twentieth century, with its unprecedented evil, its monumental wickedness.

During the Discoed repairs, they found many skeletons in the chancel – shepherds and ladies, boys and girls, and babies, of course. Short-lived folk for the most part. Short-lived, too, were the majority of the holocaust victims. Long-lived now are most of us. Traherne got all his work done at 37.

On the train to Paddington it is half-term, and the children talk like birds. We are a travelling cage in Oxfordshire. Outside, nothing much is going on. I see Traherne riding his horse from Credenhill to Brasenose College, he at least bursting with joy. He is one of the rare seventeenth-century poets who made an inventory of his nursery, his drum, 'a peny'. He describes his brother Phillip's relief at finding the same moon wherever he happens to be.

Canon Ellerton was similarly comforted in his 'The day thou gavest, Lord, is ended', only by the sun.

Making Money like the Bee

THIS MORNING, as the first cold rains of autumn rattled the window, I heard an especially fine Thought for the Day. It was by the Rt Revd James Jones, the Bishop of Liverpool. He had discovered a salutary verse in George Herbert's lengthy poem 'Providence' for dealing with, or at least saying something wise about, the banking crash.

Herbert was a considerable naturalist and dietician. Here is what Bishop Jones quoted from 'Providence', relating it to the vast financial disorder in which the world now finds itself:

Bees work for man; and yet they never bruise
Their master's flowers, but leave it, having done,
As fair as ever, and as fit to use;
So both the flower doth stay, and honey run.

Wall Street worked for itself, and, having done, left it unfit for use. I remember walking along it and seeing litter and dust blowing between its high palaces, but feeling the excitement of it. Hollywood, as well as the business schools, had given it glamour. Now the world knows that it was a kind of madhouse.

The founding fathers of North America never left the divine provider out of their calculations. And so we have Providence, Kentucky; Providence, Rhode Island; Providence, Utah; Providence Mountains, etc. It is something that neither religion nor science would ever do – leave out 'the giver of all good things', whether we call it God or Nature.

Long before Christ, there was a body of writings known as *The Pali Canon*, and in it I discovered the following:

The wise and moral man
Shines like a fire on a hilltop,
Making money like the bee,
But does not hurt the flower.

Antony, who keeps bees in his Yorkshire vicarage garden, brings me honey. 'But,' he says, 'my bees are sick.' Bees everywhere are mysteriously suffering and dying. Should there be no more bees, we, too, may die; for our health descends from them.

Just two of them sway on the last balsam flowers. Have they come from the Cousins or Rodgers hives? I was about to pull up all the balsam in my great October clearance, but I am glad I didn't.

These are honeybees, who are the most highly organized of the social bees. They look perfect. But what about their relations, the solitary bees? Are they in full happy buzz, the carpenter bees, the leafcutter bees, the homeless bees, the mining bees, and the yellow-faced bees? Pray Providence they are.

Last Sunday, as we were keeping St Michael and All Angels, I spoke of angels, and we sang 'It came upon the midnight clear'. There is a bookish incident in Revelation which I love. It is about bitter-sweetness. John sees an angel holding a little book. The angel stands with one foot in the sea and one foot on the land, as he acknowledges the divine creation.

God then tells John to take the little book from the angel.

The angel says, 'Take it and eat it up.' When he did so, it was sweet as honey in his mouth and bitter in his belly.

The other John, down by the river, had lived on honeycomb.

OCTOBER

Constance

IT IS GETTING on for midnight, and my sister telephones from near Sydney. She is sure that it is teatime in England. How is Australia coping with the collapse of capitalism? She hadn't heard about it. She must have been driving home from listening to *Don Giovanni* at the Opera House.

I thought of us as children on our bike-rides. At a certain spot she would jump off, sit on the bank, and say: 'You go on. I'll be all right.' So on I would go, on and on through the limitless Suffolk lanes.

In New South Wales, she once drove me to where D. H. Lawrence wrote *Kangaroo* and *The Boy in the Bush*, and we sat on the hot rocks above the crashing sea where he had sat, imagining these novels blowing about in the dry Pacific wind. Behind him in the flimsy yet lasting house lurked Frieda, homesick.

My sister and I are bonded by books. At Yowie Bay, she would pile her 'musts' by my bedside. How lucky she is to be in all that warm weather! 'No, it is chilly. Only 16.'

Harvest-festival evensong at Wormingford, with the ringers in full flight and the lovely bell music filling the valley, and the tower captain calling above the sacred din. About a score of us sing the service without the organ and say the General Thanksgiving together.

There having been a Fun Day the day before, I politely ask that a scarecrow in a surplice be removed from the pulpit before I climb into it. Teddy bears had abseiled the Saxon tower, and the churchyard was hilarious. But now, alternately engaged in Psalm 122, we said: 'I was glad when they said unto me: we will go into the house of the Lord.'

There is homemade bread on the altar, and everywhere sumptuous autumn flowers, our best apples and cauliflowers, sheaves saved from the combine, and that immortal smell of enclosed vegetation and ancient stone. Sardine tins and the like prevent my final kneeling in the sanctuary, and Martha, laden with plates, looks at me understandingly from her window. 'Such is life,' she says. 'You can't get to the holiness for the baked beans.'

I pot the tender plants and take them in ere the winter storms begin. This is a big job. It is so mild that they look surprised. But one sudden frost and they will blacken and die. They will spend the winter looking out of the larder window, rather lost as we are when we are out of our element.

The brick-floored old room will brew up a rich aroma of jam, onions, and geraniums, plus a heady reek of wine. 'By February, it will knock you back a bit,' says a neighbour. Bemused birds will alight on the sill and look in, then tap against the glass, their beaks providing percussion for the draining fridge. Now and then the white cat makes an inspection, sidling between the jars, weaving her way through the bottles, disturbing nothing.

Strangers call. Also my publisher. I should have given them real coffee. I do give them real answers; for it is the least I can do. I might be out of Mocha, but I must not be out of what they want to know. They fear they are disturbing my peace. That they are men from Porlock. Far from it, I want to insist. How could silence or solitude be experienced if they were not interrupted now and then?

'Elected Silence, sing to me!' cried the teenaged Gerard Manley Hopkins, romantically choosing a monk's cell. He then filled it with marvellous-sounding words.

Little Easton

ROLLING back the carpet of ash and hazel leaves to make way for a vast fall of oak leaves, I find snowdrops pricking into light. It is warm. Orange sunshine splinters through the trees.

I am trying to eliminate Lancelot Andrewes from my head so that I can make space for garden matters. I had been writing about him, reading his sparky sermons, seeing him taking strings of chattering schoolboys, including George Herbert, on learned walks along the Thames path. A swaying, shouting green woodpecker drives him away.

On Sunday, after Evensong for the Five Parishes at Little Easton, devouring chocolate cake in the Bouchier chapel, we debated the meaning of dates such as 'Died 172[2/3]' on the handsome floor tablet. It was the changeover from the Julian Calendar, thought some. I said it was because this person had died in his sleep, though whether before or after midnight had been the question.

Sir Henry's large family kneel along his tomb, children

who grew up, children who perished, the latter holding their skulls. There is a sumptuous plaque to Ellen Terry by Alfred Gilbert, who made the Eros for Piccadilly, and a décolleté bust of Lady Warwick, the mistress of Edward VII.

Far away in time and attitude in true fresco on the nave wall sits a marvellous unnamed Apostle; below him the only surviving Labour of the Months. Also the rail at which I knelt for my confirmation.

We had arrived in thin but drenching rain, the main road hissing with the Sunday supermarket shoppers' cars, a sight that always brings out a latent sabbatarianism in me. What a horrible way to spend a Sunday. But soon we were passing Thomas Ken's old rectory, and ancient houses standing in the path of Stansted's new runway.

And soon I was giving out the processional hymn, and wondering what John Barnett, a rector from long ago, would have thought of my doing so. For the Good Friday Three Hours, he would have his Steinway grand brought to the church. An enormous figure in caped robes held at the throat by a pair of silver lions gnawing a chain, he would play Bach cantatas. No words. Silences and music.

My poet-friend James Turner and I would sit there under the wall paintings seeing the people wander in and out on tiptoe. In his 'Good Friday Music at Little Easton' he wrote:

We shall rejoice that the sealed Tomb
Is no longer sealed.
Our music celebrates the High Wood of Golgotha,
And the Tree

Shall blaze with its Five Wounds
Over Creation

'High Wood', I might add, was where we played as
children, a scrap of Suffolk's wildwood, dense, unmanaged,
a bit fearsome at times. A pheasant would screech up from
nowhere, a fox look at us through brambles. Or a
gamekeeper chase us. Or lovers would lie still as we passed.
A lot happened in High Wood, including ourselves, of
course.

And very soon Advent will happen, I think, as I start on
clearing the dead sticks, leaving those with the best
seedheads, making spaces.

Salisbury People, Essex Folk

TO SALISBURY, to be briefly with the dear ones there,
Alison and Judy. One should have pockets of friends here,
there, and everywhere. The weather rainy, with small
allowances of sun; the countryside between stations
empty, unpeopled. An hour with the composer Alec Roth
in George Herbert's rectory, a few minutes at his altar
across the road. The minuscule relics, a tile which says GH
1632, a door which he opened and closed. Then to Wilton,
to talk about him to the Prayer Book Society. Then a
circular glimpse of the Earl of Pembroke's palace,
with Marcus Aurelius high on his horse at the entrance.

Back to Bottengoms. The Saturday Underground shining
with clubbers and lovers. The night pulled-in near Woking,

so that when at last I arrive at my orchard, its only illumination is the white cat, fuming below a pear tree.

On Monday, a curious happening. At a grand dinner to raise funds for the Campaign to Protect Rural England, the guest on my left says that her name is Teresa Salisbury. Or was, before she married. When I tell her that I have just come from Salisbury, she tells me about an English teacher at Keele University who taught her George Herbert, and that if she ever came to church it would be because of him. A line or two of him hangs in her head – she quotes, uncertainly, 'The Collar', while all around us 100 guests roar their way through the courses.

We are in a great Tudor room. Tudor songs are sung by a choir. This huge hospitable space was no more than the brick gatehouse to a mansion which would never be built, its young lord dying before his vast enterprise could be completed.

Holiday homes are raffled. The day departs through a tall window. In the nearby church, in one of my most loved wall-paintings, St Christopher will be forever carrying his Lord across an Essex stream, while on its bank a lad, unaware of this, will be forever fishing.

My pre-dinner speech (I thought it was to be after-dinner) extols the Essex marshes, and the wild tulips at Panfield, but most of all John Ray, the botanist, son of the Black Notley blacksmith, and England's Linnaeus. Tom drives me home via Lord Marney's leaning oaks. Sometimes, conversion comes through a sliver of Herbert – a cutting from his complex acceptance of 'my Joy, my Love, my Heart', no more.

Keith will soon be here to paint the house. He is working

his way round the village. I will be his autumn task. White windows and walls the colour of the pots that they dig up on the archaeological site. He will unhook the roof-high climbers and fix a knocker to the door. No expense shall be spared. The brick sills upon which the whole structure balances will be covered with pitch, the slate plaque to John Nash RA and his wife Christine will be wiped, the grapevine slimmed down. And who will see it? A rider-by. A walker-past. A caller now and then. Certainly no one in a bus. Another Tom in his aeroplane, godlike above my trees, will look down on me. This is only right.

Lesley Leggett, our master bell-ringer, has gone his way. No more his changes, his peals, his flying tunes, his mathematical worship. For countless Sundays he rung among the brass knights. I see him in his place.

Dean Frances Elizabeth

ST LUKE'S little summer burns into the study. Various birds are making helicopter pauses in mid-air to get at the mullein seeds. Keith has finished painting the old farmhouse and we top out with a glass of port. He has fixed the Hadleigh door-knocker, and no longer will visitors have to bang with their hands like desperate shelter-seeking men in a Hammer horror film.

The Tudor brick sill on which the timber frame balances has been pitched a shiny black. Keith and I stand in the garden and stare, overcome with admiration. That evening, a deer comes to the orchard to stand still in the falling leaves, a delicate living piece of heraldry. Neither do I move. How long are we to keep this up? I wonder. Then, in a few high leaps, it is gone. Hornets continue to find themselves the wrong side of the pane and buzz like motorbikes. Can we sing Rawnsley's

> Loved physician! for his word
> Lo, the Gospel page burns brighter,
> Mission servant of the Lord,
> Painter true, and perfect writer.

I imagine a portrait by him turning up at Sotheby's. After all, the mysterious Theophilus made sure that his books remained in print. And how magnificent to be a physician of the soul. As for his travel writing – that scary voyage to Malta – it is like something out of Homer's *Odyssey*, deceptive landfalls and all. In his day it was 'All aboard for terror!'

Vicki from the farm up the road has just flown to Athens in a couple of hours for her nephew's Greek Orthodox baptism, and no doubt reading all the way, the same jewel-like Aegean islands glittering below her. He will be called Leonidas after the brave king of Sparta, the accent on the third syllable.

Christopher and I drive to Bury St Edmunds for the installation of Frances Elizabeth as Dean of the Cathedral. And on the same day as the Bishop of Fulham and the Folkestone parish announce their flight to Rome. Of what small consequence this is in the light of heaven and the starry firmament on high.

We lay canons occupy distant stalls and the Installation

reaches us in glorious bursts. Heaven is down there in the nave where bishops and mayors galore, plus the lovely choir, act out the fine liturgy. Walton's *Jubilate*; Gerald Finzi's setting of Edward Taylor's

> Methinks I see Heaven's sparkling courtiers fly,
> In flakes of Glory down him to attend,
> And hear Heart-cramping notes of Melody
> Surround his Chariot as it did ascend.

My goodness! In the car park, sunset glorified the belching chimney of the sugar-beet factory and the finials of the cathedral tower alike. That evening, I re-read a favourite poem about the Kingdom, Vachel Lindsay's 'General William Booth enters into Heaven'.

> Booth died blind, and still by faith he trod,
> Eyes still dazzled by the ways of God.

Whom will I see there, we might pause to ask, the Lord being so eclectic. And so unlike us.

Ruth and Tess

A TEMPEST of autumn-cleaning has hit the ancient house. Beginning in a modest way, with a reordering of the larder – a long room that began its days as the farm dairy – it swept on until rotten window-frames were exchanged with Simon the joiner's perfect replacements, and Keith arrived with paint and ladders, and I, not to be outdone, with a fine brass door-knocker. The October sun shone with some enthusiasm, and the ash leaves began to sail down.

To conclude matters, David, a gardener who knows what he is doing, swept aside my sentimentality and lopped a gawky shrub down to size, opening up a new view. The white cat, who loves action in others, purred throughout. The first free morning when brushes and saws had vanished, a hare came to the lilac tree and stared around.

The Kestrel potatoes have been lifted and placed in a dark box. They scrub up a delicate pink, and may see me through to March. The air smells of lifted onions, miles and miles of them, and also of the mere hint of decay. There is something satisfying about all things passing, even us. Considering the appalling things many of us achieve in a comparatively brief existence, what a mercy it is that we must go.

A crocodile of ramblers swing over the hill, and a muntjac makes himself heard in the thinning wood. October. Hornets have to be let out of the bedrooms. I have never quite discovered how they get in. They rage against the glass, threatening all hell. None shall harm you, I promise. Have I not sent you on your furious way this many a year? You should be nesting in a hollow tree, not in a red-brick palace behind my vine. You have got above yourselves, great wasps.

But, they buzz, we are social wasps, and can do you great service in the kitchen, if only you did not go mad at the sight of us. And we would not waste our mighty sting on the likes of you – unless, of course, you try our patience. Your invention of glass is a great trial to us: to see our world, and not to enter it; what a mystery. To die in the attempt: how heroic, how pitiful. But what a way to treat a guest. You should be ashamed.

I preach on Ruth and Tess, women of the field. In the Old Testament story, three husbands die leaving three widows. Two of them, Naomi and her daughter-in-law, Ruth, return to Bethlehem, the House of Bread, having nowhere else to go, the foreign adventure having collapsed. 'Call me Mara' – 'bitter' – says the older woman, expecting the cold shoulder. Only to find that her dead husband's fields have been cultivated and kept in waiting for his return.

As for Ruth, the humble gleaner, Bethlehem's corn is not alien for long, and her harvest is young Boaz. So all is well, not to say glorious; for their descendant would be none other than the Christ, son of David, descendant of a Gentile and a Jew. 'In Christ there is neither Jew nor Gentile,' Paul would say.

Alien elements both disturbed and enriched Thomas Hardy's Wessex. Those who saw the English countryside as 'contented' found him upsetting. He read and re-read the book of Ruth, one and two Samuel, and one and two Kings. They were his favourites. Today's harvest festivals are drained of all common experience. The sheaves are so near yet so elusive. 'Plenty' is now something quite else.

Old Growth, New Players

MY NEIGHBOUR Jonathan Doe, 'Hedgecutting Specialist', is paying his destructive visit. And thank goodness, for the ancient farm-track is all but obliterated by growth. Tangles of weed had begun to hold hands over it, and sagging boughs to canopy above it. But now, thanks to the 'murderer' – i.e. Jonathan's cutter – a most probably Saxon road appears, broad and enticing. Who would not walk to the river?

Once a year, this time in the midst of harvest, the growth parts like the Red Sea, and travellers to the house can bump down to me in their cars without a scratch. On one side, the flax, once a pure blue and now a sullen green, and, opposite, the grazing pastures where Jean's horses feed now become distinctive lands. Baby partridges and rabbits scuttle between the two, mad for cover.

Behind the farmhouse, owing to spring clearance, a forest of Himalayan balsam, ten feet high, sways with insects. Nettles thrive. Birds call – including a hidden blackcap with his operatic song. Shall I leave this weed paradise for another week? I finger the blade of Roger's lovely scythe, and try not to feel like Madame Defarge. The blackcap sings, 'Not yet! Not yet!' Jonathan says, 'Have you noticed how the evenings are pulling in?' Darkness falls at nine o'clock. But the mornings stay early, and the Grove geese fly over at 7 a.m. sharp.

To my joy, I find a Henry James novel that I haven't read, *The Ambassadors*, and sit outside in the sun, my whole being slowed down by his prose. The friends from small-town America are spreading their wings in Paris. Young and not so young, they learn to fly. But not too quickly, thank heaven; for it would be unendurable for a Henry James novel not to last. The white cat joins me, pushing her snowy head on to the page. And thus we sit as we forget the floods and the cuts for an hour or two every afternoon, not to mention the demands of the Man Booker Prize. A delight fills me as I realize that my shelves are fat with old paperbacks waiting to surprise me.

Christopher and I go to Snape to hear the National Youth Orchestra, and to look across the marshes to Iken. The orchestra is exuberant, enchanting, and numerous, layers of players receding out of sight. Next stop the Albert Hall. We park by the Alde where, in my day, as they say, the lighters bore the malt away on the tide. And now these musicians, these audiences, this rustling of the reeds, this flat view that St Botolph meditated on. And, for me, these ghosts in the brick opera-box – Ben, Peter, and Imo – so empty now.

A buoyant Russian conductor puts the boys and girls through their paces, and receives not much less than adoration, and we clap him like mad. The next morning, in church, we sing John Bunyan's answer to the horrors of the world, his defiance of all that it throws against us, its 'dismal stories'. Today's journalists see that we never go without these, although their very plenitude somehow hardens our hearts. I feel that I should feel more, and even pray that I will feel more. And write cheques. And insert the latest tragedies into the petitions on a Sunday. But I am not like, say, Dr Karen Woo. Few of us are.

Is Your Worship all it Should Be?

THE DAYS are perfectly sad. Leaves mulch; skies are neither light nor dark. There are plants that have lost all sense of time, and as such are living dangerously, like my budding hollyhocks and yuccas, which will flower in the first frost.

If we are at all downcast, it is because we have ceased to love melancholy. There are those who drug themselves so that they can live on a high, and there are those who re-read wondrous books such as *The Anatomy of Melancholy* so that they can live on a low. Live richly, that is.

Robert Burton wrote this indispensable book in 1621, throwing off wonderful squibs of learning and literary delights in all directions. And apparently without effort. Everyone loved it.

Here are a few of his treasures. Did he find them or invent them? 'Women wear the breeches.' 'All poets are mad.' 'Cookery is become an art, a noble science, cooks are gentlemen.' 'Why doth one man's yawning make another yawn?' 'Aristotle said melancholy men of all others are most witty.' 'Many things happen between the cup and the lip.' 'Birds of a feather gather together.' 'Ignorance is the mother of devotion.'

If I dare say so, this last epithet tumbled into my head when I read about the flight to Rome of certain Anglican priests; for if they had really understood or comprehended the beauty and truths of Anglican Christianity, they would have stayed put and practised them, to the benefit of the Church everywhere.

And the Church of England itself needs to take a critical look at its 'worship'; for some of what goes on now under this description is beyond belief.

Most people's worship involves going to church for one hour a week. This should be 'something different' from all the other hours, something profound, moving, and intensely spiritual. No fooling about. 'We love the place, O God, Wherein thine honour dwells.' Let us love it better.

Melancholic owls call all night across the river. Lying in bed at six in the morning, I listen to their cries. As did the early wakers in this same room, when Robert Burton was adding to his enchanting compendium. There is hard-to-reach dust on the beam above my head, and a trapped hornet beats against the window. I let it out into the owl universe.

Chilly dawn air comes in like a knife. Leaves choke the gutter, and a spiral of rainwater hits the border. The white cat is outside and looking up – as we should all do. And somebody rides past. Well, I never.

I read some more Burton. He calls a tulip a 'tulipant', and calls a wanderer a 'landleaper'. One lives and learns. I must do some landleaping in the direction of Heather's shop. But breakfast first. Baked pears, piles of toast, proper coffee. Young soldiers die on the News; the dreadful bankers carry on regardless, no lessons having been learnt. Incomprehensible amounts of money pile up in my ancient kitchen. One of the reasons why the money-men get away with it, and some of the politicians, too, is that we – I – have no idea what they are talking about.

Yet the sad-happy autumn morning spreads itself over the already greening fields. And we, having done our stint, are going to see Britten's *Turn of the Screw*. And so it would have been in 1621: work, play, religion, weather.

'What have we come to?'

THE LEAVES are falling fast now. They descend in companionable flurries, and we walk on wet gold. You can see through the hedges. The stone-hard Warden pears, too, will tumble down any minute now, and I must get to them before the rabbits take their bite.

St Luke; and an intermittent sun does its best for him. At Little Horkesley, I have a 'Matins for the Feast of St Luke', solemn and holy, and see him delivering his scrolls to the mysterious Theophilus. How frequently the New Testament name-drops, and then says no more.

I take David to see the telescopic font-cover at St Gregory's, Sudbury. I sat under it in my youth, listening to Canon Hughes. It is still a little gaudy, with medieval paint, but the Apostles have long left their canopies. David has been reading the latest William Boyd novel on 'Book at Bedtime' and, seated on the nave chairs, we talk softly about reading aloud.

It is almost my favourite thing – to be read to. When I lie dying, will somebody read to me? Shall I leave some suggestions? Poems by Hardy or Cavafy, Chekhov's short stories, the Book of Psalms? Make a note.

David and I move to the chancel to try out Archbishop Simon's misericords (mercy), tipping them up and lodging our bottoms on the slippery ledge. Beneath one of them is a nice carved dog, the very one that lay at his feet and that now flies high on the municipal flag.

On Market Hill, the traders no longer shout as they once did, and the town is subdued and yet busy.

An autumnal wait at the bus stop. Two old women.

'They've put it in, then?'

'Last month. The noise! Bang, bang!'

'Does it have a glow?'

'No glow.'

'Pity. We know there's no heat in a glow, but it's psychologic.'

'Oh, how I loved my coal fire! Oh, how I loved its heat! To sit staring at pipes all evening – what have we come to?'

Richard Mabey arrives to have one of our long tramps 'under trees'. The valley has far more trees than it did when John Constable painted it, and it is quite hard to see out from his favourite perch on Gun Hill. But he would have adored how it is now, the Stour so bright, the farms so white.

We come home along an abandoned lane full of dead wood and badgers' droppings, but indelibly marked by men's feet. Trodden is the word. Here and there, the mushrooms. Above, the teatime sky. We encounter Neal, the Suffolk Wildlife Trust friend, and talk about owls.

The valley is full of owls – always was. It is owl country. Neal awards me a feather from a barn-owls' nest 'to put on your mantelpiece'. He and Richard discuss black poplars; for this is black poplar country, too. And the grey-yellow October afternoon dwindles into sunset.

A notice on a gate says 'Bull', and we are halfway across the meadow when we see that it is true. It is teatime for bulls, too, however, and he grazes greedily in the distance. The lees of summer flowers – scabious, burnet saxifrage – bloom in the lane. Burnet means the Old French burnete – dark brown.

And thus home, to a white cat who walks by herself,

sometimes high up in the orchard trees. The guests gone, I read to myself.

Roger Deakin

IT IS BEFORE dawn, and dark. Very soon, the masses of hazel which I have let grow will filter-in the day. Each winter, I wave my saw at them, then see their stumpy catkins, and reprieve them for another year. I tell them: 'Coppicing is good for you' – and their boughs shine.

It is St Luke's little summer, and he is doing us proud with his warm sunshine and soft winds. I imagine him carrying his Gospel scrolls to the most excellent Theophilus, his publisher, saying: 'Make a good job of it.'

Roger's *Notes From Walnut Tree Farm* arrives in the post, and there we both are, setting off to Tiger Hill, he in his big boots and big black coat, tall and bursting with health. Although not so. His dust and the brown-red dusty bark of the old pears in the orchard are one.

He would arrive unexpectedly, looming into my low rooms, happy and expectant like a dog. Where shall we go? What shall we do? His *Notes* answers these questions. Reading them, I feel more deserted than at his funeral. He was so dead there, and he is so alive on the page.

Here is what I said. Here is what we did. Here is the white cat listening. All this week, she has opted to make a bed in the rope-box, purring thunderously on the uncomfortable, one would think, coils. Maybe she has ancestors who joined the Navy: ships' cats who mucked in with sailors and saw the world. Roger's cats are all over the place in his book, on the Aga, by the moat.

Thinking of him reminds me of the scythe that he brought from Stowmarket. And this reminds me that it is a good day to cut the tall seeding plants in the orchard, the frail horsetail and tall hogweed. I have to keep the scythe high enough to avoid the primroses and cowslips. I am writing about Thomas Traherne. Every now and then, thinking of a good bit, I hurry indoors to put it down.

How Traherne adored being outside! He said that he would have liked to lie under a tree all day – all his days – wearing a leather suit, and doing absolutely nothing except thank God for letting him see the earth. As he was the rector, however, he had work to do. And, as it was in the seventeenth century, there was theology to rail about. But, like Roger, he had to put himself on to the page.

I have always suspected that much of Traherne's immortal *Centuries of Meditations* was scribbled in the open air. He is the singer of human happiness. His prose is so intoxicating that it makes one unsteady on one's feet.

We are off to Felixstowe to have lunch with Ina. Old Felixstowe is the scene of the most frightening ghost story in the language, M. R. James's 'O whistle and I'll come to you, my lad'. New Felixstowe was the seaside for gentlefolk. The crunchy shingle will make the waves hiss as they slap their way through it, and possibly St Luke's sun will take the chill off it.

St Felix sailed from Burgundy to Suffolk to convert us. In 631, he was made Bishop of Dunwich, setting up a fine school for boys. Dunwich has been washed away but its bishopric is undrowned – is as dry and bright as a bone.

Will we have time after lunch to see Dunwich crumbling away? No. Roger would have said yes. He said yes to everything.

NOVEMBER

Cambridge: Siegfried Sassoon

WITH THE CLOCK going back, and All Souls' looming, I always sense a moody suspension of time. An hour is lost in order to gain an hour; the dead yet living briefly retake their vacated seats in the ancient church. It is unutterably sad, say what you will. Neither spooky nor made endurable by tomfoolery, but just sad. The commemoration of All Souls' came from Cluny, as did so many extraordinary things.

I like to imagine that St Odilo, who invented it, noted that certain faces, often young, failed to appear in that grand liturgy each autumn, and that he became their remembrancer. As, indeed, we do, as we hear a long list of the recent dead. The fearful 'Dies Irae' was sung (though not now), and the living would quake. Early in the morning, I watch wild formations of seagulls fly low across the new ploughing, and the sky gradually lightening from fading black to gold.

On Tuesday, we went to see the Siegfried Sassoon exhibition at Cambridge University Library. It rained, and leaves fell all the way. Wet, ebony lanes; soaked joggers. I was not prepared for the poet's minuscule hand as I pored over the showcases. The writing became smaller and smaller as the years progressed, and the later pages seemed to have been written with a mapping pen. I never get over seeing the first draft of a famous poem. Tiny beyond expectation, here is 'Everyone sang'.

Everyone suddenly burst out singing;
And I was filled with such delight
As prisoned birds must find in freedom,
Winging wildly across the white
Orchards and dark-green fields; on – on – and out of
  sight.

The repetition of visionary matters. I bump my nose from case to case in the preservative gloom as I try to make out Sassoon's hand. His Great War is reflected on the TV screen as the newsmen don their poppies. I recall a visit he made to Thomas Hardy.

'He showed me a "new old" poem, "On Stinsford Hill at Midnight", and told me how he saw a girl singing alone one night as he returned home (a Salvationist girl who died soon after). She had a tambourine (he called it "a timbrel" in the poem). The poem leaves the reader to decide whether it was a live woman or a ghost.'

I once sat in the room where Sassoon talked to Hardy. I was helping to edit the New Wessex edition of Hardy's works. I can't remember if it was late in the year, but I can never forget the immense haunting of Max Gate since then – the clock-sounding rooms, the dull garden, the enchanted melancholy, the 'presence'.

Hardy, wrote Sassoon in his almost invisible hand, 'never sits in the comfortable chair or on the sofa, but perches himself on a straight-backed chair, and leans his head lightly on his hand, in an easy attitude, dignified and self-possessed and calm'.

To evensong in Selwyn College Chapel in a kind of dream. Young souls – like the Lord himself.

'We are as clay in the Potter's hand'

ALL SOULS. 'Have you a soul?' I ask the white cat. We stare at each other enigmatically. I read out the names of the departed in two churches, filling the pews. The rains have blown themselves out, and we are engulfed in a stillness that fits the service.

All Souls is a Benedictine remembrance from the tenth century, sombre and sad. It used to contain the tragic 'Dies Irae' sequence, which may now be omitted from the masses for the dead. Our village dead, I feel, are far from wrath. Phillip, Gordon, Joan, all of them, are with God. So I commend them to his infinite love. Pages and pages of them.

The altar candles waver. I preach on that most symbolically used ordinary vessel in the Bible – the pot. What is it that tells the archaeologist most about human history, fragmented or whole, domestic or in the Palissy or Bernard Leach class? The pot.

The potter is his Maker. God made him out of clay, and he deals with clay, fashioning it with his hands, spinning it on his wheel (like Brenda sitting opposite me in the choir, who is our potter), and firing it. 'We are in God's hands as clay in the potter's hand,' said Jeremiah.

There were claypits all around us when we were
children, brickyards where they made the famous Suffolk
Whites. Clay flowers such as coltsfoot grew in them. The
remoulding of ourselves has always been an ambition.
Omar Khayyám, that poet of the pot, wrote:

Ah, Love! could Thou and I with Fate conspire
To grasp this sorry Scheme of Things entire,
Would not we shatter it to bits – and then
Re-mould it nearer to the Heart's Desire!

Edward FitzGerald, his translator, once lived just down the
lane from me. His was an odd, lovable life. When he died,
they put on his gravestone: 'It is He that hath made us, and
not we ourselves.' Maiden-hair grasses and dog daisies blew
all around it. No 'Dies Irae' thundered through his earthly
existence, just genius and gossip.

It has been book-signing time, and I have travelled to
foreign parts – Powys and Norfolk – writing 'With kind
wishes' or 'With love' to strangers and friends. Yellow
leaves stuck to car windows, and the tarmac shone.

It was late at night when Richard Mabey drove through
Thetford forest, braking now and then to glimpse a deer.
We talked shop. The huge comfort of old friendships. The
big car hissed in the darkness. Polly and I quoted old East
Anglican saws. 'I went all the way to Swaffham to do a day's
thrarshin'.' . . . Midnight cocoa and then bed. And back to
Bottengoms in torrential rain.

After, or between, All Souls, matins and evensong, I got
the ladder out and tidied up the vine. You strip the long
stalks off in November, and cut back to the third bud in

January, when the sap is low. A handful of soggy grapes still hung from it.

This south wall is so high that I have to use the extension ladder. And the afternoon is so gloomy that I have to take care not to cut my telephone off. Pots tumble about in my head. God's creation goes beyond its basic materials, I decide. A pot may be made of clay, but it becomes more than clay. The divine Potter sees to that. I hope I will remember these brilliant thoughts by the time I get to church.

The Pet Shop Boy

LISTENING to the early-morning news, one can only conclude that many of those who get named in it are either very wicked or simply daft. Which omits most of us.

Anyway, as Borrow's philosophical Gypsy friend insisted, 'There's night and day, brother, both sweet things, sun, moon and stars, brother, all sweet things, there's likewise a wind on the heath, brother, who would wish to die?'

And there is a primrose light streaking along Duncan's hill and filtering through my tall hazel, which, every February, gets a coppicing reprieve. For no sooner do I take the saw to it than this pale light floods my memory. And so it stays, growing taller and taller, and thus more able to deal with the autumn dawn.

I have been writing about Lancelot Andrewes and reading his court sermons, the ones James I had to listen to about five times a year. Including Gunpowder Day. The

King was torn between being overwrought by this visiting bishop, and being excited by what he was about to hear. For he loved a good sermon. And he loved being told that he was divine. And he loved having the new Bible named after him.

Andrewes had translated Genesis to 2 Kings, although neither he nor the other committees so much as mentioned William Tyndale, the real genius of the English Bible. But I like Lancelot Andrewes for his seeming indifference to pomp and circumstance, and the way he walked through life.

Unmarried, uncomfortable, but not uncomforting, he used a teaching method at Westminster School which I have always admired. It was to take the boys out of their smelly classroom and crocodile them along the Thames path, telling them wonders in his Suffolk voice. One of the boys was George Herbert.

To Sudbury, our Waitrose shrine. Thomas Gainsborough stands on his plinth, soaked to his bronze skin. In the pet shop, buying a bird-feeder, I suddenly realize that I have been here before. I am a child, with Mother, and the shelves are filled with hanks and skeins of wool and silk, and she is stroking them on the counter and debating how many ounces she will need. There are embroidery patterns, knitting needles, and fragile chairs on which to balance, and a large woman who reminds me of the sheep-shopkeeper in *Alice*.

And now there are bins for nuts, and cages, and iron legs for the bird-feeder, and an aroma that would send the white cat wild. And a pet shop boy who prescribes the correct diet for yellowhammers, etc. The rain lashes down outside.

'Is trade good?' I ask.

'Pretty good.'

'Good,' I say. Banks may crash, mortgages dry up, but birds will be watched.

I am so excited by what I have bought that I want to erect it outside the kitchen window the minute I get home, but the afternoon light drains away, and the garden grows black.

The feast of St Edmund, our local saint, approaches. The legendary spot of his coronation is visible from my bedroom window. He was 15, a kind of river prince, I have always imagined, being rowed up the Stour, Waveney, Yare, learned, holy, getting ready for his immortality at Bury St Edmunds. Murdered at 29. His vast abbey reduced to a kind of flint abstraction, its roots softened by carpet-bedding. Andrewes would have known about him.

Barbara Pym

DANK DAYS. Mulch. Slanting rains. The first leaf-carpet is ash and aspen. The latter's grand name is *Populus tremula* from the trees' trembling in the wind, but now their music is reduced to a squelching under my feet. Scores of seagulls wheel fretfully over the hill, presumably searching for something better than horse leavings; for they rarely descend.

The atmosphere is richly sad – pensive. No humans about. Does the ancient farmland mourn its labourers? Just David now, who seeds and reaps it, slashes its hedges into shape with 'the murderer', and commands it from on high.

Our faith, like most faiths, is drawn out of pastorality, out of agriculture, out of days like these, when mud and rottenness, wet feet, and cold hands had to meet as part of the bargain.

A dizzy climber on the east wall breaks its strings and falls flat, which allows me to give it a good back and sides before tying by the door. My ladder sinks before settling, as we all must, I suppose. (You see what a wet November afternoon does to the spirit.)

Tugging off my boots, I might read a favourite Barbara Pym, *A Few Green Leaves*. She wrote this lively novel on her deathbed, and when she was writing to me about the reception of T. S. Eliot into the Church of England, which took place in her village church on 29 June 1917, St Peter's Day. It was Finstock, Oxfordshire, Barbara's own church. Here the doors were locked before Tom had the waters of regeneration poured over his head in the presence of his godfathers, B. H. Streeter and Vere Somerset.

Barbara thought that the following lines from 'Little Gidding' might refer to this mighty episode in the Church of England:

Thus, love of a country
Begins as attachment to our own field of action
And comes to find that action of little importance
Though never indifferent. History may be servitude,
History may be freedom. See, now they vanish,
The faces and places, with the self which, as it could,
   loved them,
To become renewed, transfigured, in another
   pattern.

In *A Few Green Leaves*, Tom the Rector finds Miss Lee 'doing what she called "her" brasses'. He also finds, to his shame, that the lectern is not brass but oak, and that although he had been in the parish for years, he had noticed the polishing but not what was being polished. Did Miss Lee sometimes regret that it was not a brass lectern? 'Oh, no, Rector, I love that old wooden bird, and I love polishing it. A brass one may look more brilliant, but wood can be very rewarding, you know . . .'

Our lectern at Wormingford is made of wood, and was carved by Joliffe Tufnell, our squire. Should this eagle fly off, it would be out of the north door. It is a mighty creature, fully armorial, non-benign, and heavy with message. The Authorized Version is spread on it, and shortish people have to mount a box to read it. A microphone carries its lessons near and far.

Mr Clegg is the gamekeeper in *A Few Green Leaves*, and one is grateful for it. There are no flying bishops, only flying words, not all of them kind. The dark afternoon falters and streaky yellow bands are coldly illuminating for an hour or so.

DECEMBER

King Jesus

SOON IT WILL be Christ the King, a recognition which begins in tomfoolery and continues in real majesty. Jesus himself makes no claims. He simply stands before us. The feast itself is new. Pope Pius XI proclaimed it in 1925, and it is only from 1970 that it has been celebrated on the last Sunday before Advent, although the final 'For the Epistle' of the Book of Common Prayer, Jeremiah 23, declares, 'a King shall reign, and prosper, and shall execute judgement and justice in the earth'.

George Herbert was rationally attracted to this divine royalty, seeing Christ as his ultimate instructor. 'Teach me, my God and King.' The teachings of Jesus are elementary, yet advanced, as so many simple truths are. Herbert called his poem 'The Elixir'. In his day, an elixir was an alchemical preparation for making a sovereign remedy for prolonging life.

He comes to mind on this still December morning, because my friend Judy Rees, who cares for his church at Bemerton, has sent me 22 Herbert hymns on a disc of Sarum Voices, including Alec Roth's setting of 'The Flower', in which the Lord sets aside his crown to don a gardener's apron.

I have been bringing inside the frost-threatened plants,

lining them up in the old dairy. But no sweeping of leaves, yet. Let them finish sailing down. Bottengoms is not a tidy spot, heaven knows. And I love its annual yellowing, its whispery walks, its mulch. These things go well with my sloth. The white cat takes the hint and sleeps in the boiler-room, emerging about ten times a day for grub, love, etc. She is a republican, and what's mine is hers.

There are a nice lot of sheep about in the village, and anti-churchyard-mowers long for them to be put among the graves, as they once were. I saw this happening in Rodmell churchyard, though long ago. Virginia Woolf would have watched them. The tombstones – the better sort – were protected with wire netting, I recall. We were off to Chanctonbury Ring in June sunshine, and the Sussex Downs were rich in the wildflowers and butterflies which only sheep grazing produces.

Back home, Jean's horses balance on the hilltop, wondering whether to topple into Suffolk or Essex. I watch them through my lashes as I turn the pages.

Herbert worries about autumn. 'Brave rose, (alas!) where art thou?' He himself will leave the garden all too soon. The River Nadder will flow at its foot for ever and ever. His bidding bell will be rung by other hands. 'Soon I fled Unto my house, where to repair the strength Which I had lost.' But he could not sleep. 'I found that some had stuff'd the bed with thoughts.' He tried to pray. No good. When I slept in his rectory, I couldn't sleep for thoughts of him. 'Herbert,' I told myself, 'just the other side of the wall!'

And, now, his Kingly friend. It is his time of the year when the trees go gold. And the last roses go mushy. And the Little Owls sit on posts. It is now that his reign begins –

officially, that is. Autumn is a kind of enthronement. Sad and sumptuous, it elevates as it decays. The fields are full green in Advent, as they should be. The question is, of course: will it snow before Christmas?

What Value is it?

HEAVY FROST, they say. Ancient sheets and curtains are thrown over pelargoniums and succulents that haven't been brought inside. The following night ditto – only that when I look out the next morning, there is no frost, and I am confronted by various horticultural versions of Tracey Emin's *My Bed*.

The air is soft and rainy, and countless birds fill the far distances. I hang the damp sheets in the hot pumproom, and find pots for the outsiders. Late, late, is what I am. Always. 'You'll be late for your funeral,' they said. Reading is the problem, they said. The things they said.

One February night, his baby son sound asleep, the fire nearly out, and in an 'extreme silentness', the youthful Coleridge wrote: 'The Frost performs its secret ministry, Unhelped by any wind.' Arriving at St Edmundsbury Cathedral, I discover it doing exactly the same thing, tidying up the gardens, stinging my skin, sending the everlasting plume of smoke from the sugar-beet factory sky high.

In Coleridge's poem it is 'the night thatch' that 'Smokes in the sunthaw'. I witnessed this as a boy. And St Edmund would certainly have seen it at Bury, which was then a thatched farm. I now tell the Cathedral Guild about my 'first poet', a long-dead though for me a still-living influence, James Turner, whose houses, strewn from Suffolk to Cornwall – they were enthusiastic movers – were littered with the works of Thomas Traherne and George Herbert.

It was where I first encountered them. And where I first met with tuberculosis. Not that it was ever mentioned. It was just present, and with it its strange gift of vivid creativity to accompany the fine pallor. When he died, I was given his Traherne. Old black-and-white photos show it lying about in summer deckchairs and winter rooms.

Last week, the Traherne Society generously made me a patron. We do not know whether this wonderful prose-poet had consumption, but he left the scenes that so enchanted him, as did Herbert, in his thirties. Coleridge grew old and cranky, and was never able to regrasp the vision. Few can. It is why we take drugs – some of us. R. S. Thomas wisely watched birds in his eighties. Multitudinous birds perpetually winging between him and Holy Island. Timeless manoeuvres, screeching liturgies, endless patterns, abstract intentions, though better for the soul than afternoon television.

I have just finished a new book. It is an odd feeling. It is packed up and posted. 'What value is it?' asks the post-office lady. A judgemental voice has ordered me to counter number 21. Bumpy Christmas parcels are being weighed in the balances. The High Street sways with corporation light. Back at the ranch, I put away my second copy, my 'papers', just in time to prevent the white cat from nesting in them. The desk – the coast – is clear.

The wet garden says: 'What about me?' All in good time. I am not a perfect gardener from Bury St Edmunds. In fact, I may not lift a finger until Advent. I may put on another log and read. Heavy frosts, warns the Scottish voice, but in Scotland. There is nothing for it. The last plants must come in – must serve their sentence in the big larder window until 1 May. Else – disaster.

Learned Friends

ADVENT. The adventurous Creator enters his own creation. Antony, my gentle friend from the north, arrives in the east. Where shall we go this time? It is his turn to point the route. The weather is a yellow-grey kind of scudding skies and faintly rattling hedges. 'Norfolk,' he says. He has to pick up a fibreglass Child in Walsingham. Plus his fibreglass parents, visitors, and creatures.

My chief memory of Walsingham is of – walls. Of medieval streets and quiet reconstructions of the medieval mind. No one is there. Jesus's head peers out from the Priory gate. Are there any more pilgrims before curfew? Charles I's head tops a doorway. The trinket shops glitter. The great shrine is dark and warm, womb-like in the late afternoon.

We walk to St Mary's, so perfectly recovered by Laurence King after the inferno of 1961. It was the feast of St Camillus, a soldier of fortune who was so ruined by gambling that he had to work as a builder's labourer. He had a bad leg, and its ghastly hospital treatment made him form an order called the Servants of the Sick. St Philip Neri got him ordained by an English priest, Thomas Goldwell, in Rome. This in 1584. Had Goldwell returned to England, they could have burned him, too. A fitting day, then, for a church to catch fire.

Antony tells me all sorts of Anglo-Catholic things, and I tell him all sorts of literary-Walsingham things; thus we make a learned couple. The Child and his companions are safely packed in the back of the car. Antony tells me about 'Comper pink', and I mention a favourite poem.

> As you came from the holy land
> Of Walsinghame,
> Met you not with my true love
> By the way as you came?

It is by Sir Walter Raleigh, and is about ageing and change. It ends quite wonderfully:

> But true love is a durable fire,
> In the mind ever burning,
> Never sick, never old, never dead,
> From itself never turning.

Geese from the Wash fly overhead in whirring skeins. We drive to the Slipper Chapel, now accompanied by a vast barn of a church, and I thought of it as it must have been when princes and peasants sat in it to take off their shoes for the last mile. Antony thought that they would have hung them round their necks so that they did not get pinched while they were praying before the Virgin's miraculously transported house. More water-birds cross the darkening sky.

How wicked to sit in the car in my new shoes, socks and all. How strange to shop in Tesco at Fakenham – a building bigger than any shrine in Christendom, I imagine.

Advent. Filled with promise, filled with fear. The pilgrim lover in Raleigh's poem has his mind on other things. And my devotions on this trip, it being through coastal Norfolk, tend to take in natural history. I feel a little like R. S. Thomas on the Llyn Peninsula, watching birds, watching God.

Reading Cavafy

AFTER THE COUNTRY funeral, drinking sherry, seeing the worried widower, I murmured the usual comforting things. 'And now I will have to write the Christmas cards,' he said. I wrote mine all day, the white cat rumbling on my lap.

The cards had beautiful Renaissance paintings on one side, and Alzheimer's or Stroke on the other. Where appropriate, I added love to the official kind wishes. The frosty garden grew green and returned to white before I had finished. The recipients spread through time, ran from schoolfriends to recent acquaintances, but were mostly people who comprised my world, other writers, priests, rural society, and, of course, far-scattered relations.

Certain cards have to contain little letters or extra devotion. Some must praise the beauty of those I have already received. I used to excoriate this ritual, but now I am glad to have it; for thinking of old John in Natal, still teaching organists, I see him walking into the pub in his RAF officer's uniform. And remembering the elderly plantswoman and her brother, I see them arrive at the fancy-dress party in costumes far too old for them, and laughing away. And so I add 'love' with conviction.

Tomorrow, I shall walk to the village post office and buy 100 second-class stamps, pick up *The Times* where Peter leaves it outside Harold's, and then start on the presents, a far weightier matter.

Advent Two and evensong for three. The ancient building wavers in candlelight. Pam reads Zephaniah, and I read Luke. We sing a hymn, but say the rest, our voices rising and falling, I and the brother and sister. I talk about the cousins Jesus and John – the boys on the Christmas card – for a few minutes.

By now, whatever faint irritation we may have felt at being so deserted has disappeared. Prayer has overtaken us. A trapped silence feeds us. It is with some regret that I place a full stop to it all with the blessing. In the black churchyard we urge each other not to fall over the tombstones, most of them to John Constable's uncles and aunts. No Christmas cards for him. Maybe a pencil-sketch of a tree.

I have cleared the back of the farmhouse of its summer detritus, the sticks and soggy leaves, the elder, the nettles. Malcolm the window-cleaner arrives, and the panes shine like a coal seam. In a couple of hours, between us, we have done marvels.

In the meadow known as Lower Bottom the horses wear their winter blankets. There is early moonlight and ice in the air. I fetch the washing in from where it has been stiffening on the orchard clothesline. Night creatures are about, rats, rabbits, badgers.

On the radio, someone is reading Cavafy's amazing poem 'Ithaca', only, of course, it isn't quite the same destination. But the name resounds, like Yeats's 'Byzantium', in the ear like a longing. Like the only worthwhile journey. Like Bethlehem.

High above, in the grey-black sky, silver planes head for Calcutta with 400 passengers reading novels and drinking Cinzano and gin, or Coca-Cola, looking down at starry Norwich. They don't make a sound.

I spend a good hour looking for my Collected Cavafy poems, having tidied them away. And there is 'Ithaca' at last. We are all on the move in Advent – God, too.

Keeping Christmas

A MEDIEVAL KING would 'keep his Christmas' at Woodstock or Westminster, or wherever he happened to be. And God keeps us wherever we happen to be. 'Keep me as the apple of the eye.'

James I liked to keep his Christmas at Whitehall, a vast palace of which only Inigo Jones's Banqueting Hall remains.

Fresh from Scotland, no longer scalded by its Kirk, James was alternately entertained, if this is the description, by Lancelot Andrewes and William Shakespeare. The mighty Bishop at the beginning of the feast, the peerless writer at its end. The sermon kept to the solemn rules with a vengeance – the often disgraceful Court pulled itself together – the play, *Twelfth Night*, kept it entranced. Rarely were there such festivities as these. They were talked about for months afterwards.

In his Christmas sermon, Andrewes' learnedness would sometimes forsake him, rather as the intellectuality of the Wise Men would forsake them as they entered the stable. Like every good preacher, he knew when to abandon the script. Or, rather, he knew that there would be moments in the Gospel story when he would go to pieces. Thus there began these emotional unscripted asides in the retelling of it.

Nobody was more understanding than James, for whom the word 'Baby' was so wonderful that he went on calling his son and lover this when they were in their twenties, signing his letters to them 'Your Dad and Gossip'.

Seated below the pulpit, he heard Bishop Andrewes approaching the stable on Christmas morning with his theology pat, his severe face all set for the great occasion, his notes crackling in his hand. And then – a newborn boy! The Saviour of mankind. The preaching went out of his voice; King and Court went silent. Not a sound in the freezing chapel. But Andrewes was not in it, he was in Bethlehem.

'An infant – the infant Word – the Word without a word – the eternal Word not able to speak a word – a wonder sure . . .'

Then, almost a fortnight later, it would all end with Twelfth Night, the holiness, the feeding, the exhaustion – and the order. For the latter was strictly enforced whatever else occurred. Twelfth Night was misrule, when the sacred pattern was reversed, and rich and poor and male and female exchanged roles. It was wild. But so would the climate be until springtime, dark and cold and deathly.

For a few hours, dukes would become servants, boys become girls. Being divine, Kings couldn't become anything else, of course. James watched his Players perform *Twelfth Night*, a final Christmas entertainment which Mr Shakespeare had written especially for him, and maybe Bishop Andrewes watched it, too. Christmas had been a box of gifts, *Twelfth Night* was a box of tricks. In between were the parties and the worship. Now had come the reckoning.

It is not quite Christmas Eve, however, and neither the Boy born to be King nor the bills are with us. In the Suffolk market town, an immense conifer sways and glitters. Teenagers who haven't as yet been shown any of the wear and tear of Christmas look beautiful under the swaying lights. The clergy are looking to their laurels as they hurry from Nine Lessons to Nine Lessons, and from Midnight to Midnight.

The bells, some of them as old as Shakespeare, rock in the towers. One should long since have been surfeited with all this. How does it stay so fresh? How do babies cause one to be at a loss for words? How strange it all is.

Advent's Enchantment

I HAD HARDLY turned my back on the late afternoon when the vast, bleached Advent moon swung up in the north-east. It whitened the puddles and lit the wet fields.

The paths are darkened with sodden leaves, and rainwater dribbles from a blocked gutter.

Carry Akroyd arrives from far Northamptonshire, and we splash off to Lavenham for Sunday lunch. My boyhood lanes twist and turn through a scrubbed universe. The pub restaurants boom in and out of season.

When we walked here long ago, Lavenham was still asleep after all the toil of the Middle Ages, when the looms clattered in every cottage, the sheep were Abrahamic, and wool was gold. We visit Carry's exhibition in the wildlife gallery, where her hares and foxes slink across canvas and paper. She is mistress of the fenland nocturn and of the geometry of sluices and cuts, of measureless skies, and this end-of-the-year moon. Our mutual passion is John Clare.

For everything I felt a love,
The weeds below, the birds above.

She can actually paint that amazing second when a thousand starlings turn left, turn right, all at once. Their only human equivalent is a thousand North Korean soldiers on parade, a breathtaking drill not without its absurdity.

Carry gone, I take part in the Advent carol service at Little Horkesley. Packed church and much expectancy. The stunning Advent antiphons, the gloriously scary Advent hymns. The first and second coming, the one precipitating the other.

A painting from the Renaissance shows the Virgin

cupping one of the tiny feet in her hand. There he lies, her
– and our – Dayspring. And

> At his feet the six-winged Seraph;
> Cherubim with sleepless eye . . .

Enchantment and terror catch each other out at Advent.
When I was a child in the mighty wool-church, singing 'Let
all mortal flesh keep silence', I would imagine the painted
ceiling lifted off like the lid of a Noah's ark, and Christ
descending in glory, and Mark Fairhead rising to the
occasion on the organ.

I was generous – Christian – and would not allow for
sheep and goats. All of us, the entire congregation, even
Mrs Palmer, and certainly Canon Hughes, ceaselessly
singing 'Alleluia!' would rise to seek the joys at his right
hand. O Adonai! O Morning Star! O mysterious Advent! O
earth! O Paradise!

O longing for Christ. The words and music for Advent
often surpass for me the words and music for Christmas.
They shake the soul. They should, one feels, stay contained
within so much else that we delegate to the Age of Faith, or
just to art. But they do not – just as those of Handel's
Messiah leap from the concert platform into our very being.
Carol services are not supposed to do this, or Georgian
oratorios. They are intended to be merely dazzling
performances. These days, I mean.

Instead, a girl is pregnant with God. Creation awaits its
Creator. And the country choir sings: 'How shall I fitly
meet thee?' It is all so ravishing, so unnerving. And the
mother rocking the tiny foot in her palm, so natural.

Christmas in Cornwall

I WAS once a Christmas guest, and now I am a Christmas host. Year after year I was on the Penzance train, and those Cornish Christmases have run together into one unforgettable West Country celebration, of which I am now, possibly, the only survivor. Because when we join a friend's Christmas, we also join that of a neighbourhood. And the North Cornwall neighbourhood was, well, getting on a bit, shall we say. And I was young and petted, which was nice.

My host was the poet and novelist James Turner, and through him I would meet Charles Causley and Malcolm Arnold, chilly Cornish churches, vast empty beaches, wild pubs, roaring headlands, and an out-of-season landscape that stretches before me at this minute, untouched by time, blowy, enticing. It is only by the greatest self-restraint that I don't lock my door and set off this very minute to Paddington.

Except, when I reach Bodmin Road, the little car won't be there to meet me. And strangers will inhabit Treneague, and the other guests will be scattered, like James's dust, on Bodmin Moor, high up by the Cheesewring. And Malcolm Arnold won't be buying rounds in the Cornish Arms. Yet all this does not sadden me, because the Cornish Christmases themselves stay full of life.

Goodness knows how many of them there were. They began at Dawlish, when the train hugged the coast and the west of England ran into view. Excitement would fill me then. The tails from the brace of pheasants which my Suffolk landlord had given me would twitch on the luggage rack.

177

Then I would come to the granite bedroom, and the gulls howling outside, and James, swathed in an immense dressing-gown, with the morning tea. And the early service in the barrel-roofed church, meekly shivering on our knees. And then the presents – often of our own books. And Cathy, deploring Suffolk, would say, 'What a good thing that we discovered Cornwall. Poor you, still in that cold East Anglia.'

And then would come those local parties, each like chapters in a novel when seen from this distance. And the drives through the deep lanes in which the spring flowers already showed themselves. The days of my visit were carefully allocated, one for the Paris-Joneses, one for Charles Causley, one for me to be on my own on the thunderous cliffs. One for a girl who had christened herself Jill Holiday. Jill had a bookshop in pre-fish-restaurant Padstow.

In Padstow Church there was a memorial to Charles Dickens's friend Dr Marley, who gave his name to Scrooge's partner in spite of being quite the opposite to that man of business. Which was the joke.

Charles Causley would take us on a mystery tour, once to see the rectory of Sabine Baring-Gould at Lew Trenchard on the Devon border, and to places that only a native Cornishman would know. He had a dry wit. His life was divided between schoolmastering and caring for his invalid mother. Somehow, between these conscientiously performed tasks, would come masterpieces such as *Timothy Winters*.

And there would be the strenuous Boxing Day walks by the Atlantic. Well-fed folk and their racing dogs would wave and shout 'Happy New Year!' into the wind. It was, now I come to think of it, all very active.

'Did you have a good Christmas?' they would ask in Suffolk. 'Whew!'

'At the Yeoman's House'

THE FIRST hard frost. All nature bends before it. The ancient rooms themselves feel crisp. The white cat flies through her flap with panache to settle on the ladder-back chair for the day. She gnaws the strange white stuff from her toes. The chair is old enough for Dr Johnson to have sat on with Hodge. Boswell could not abide cats, but nor could he omit them from his masterpiece.

'I frequently suffered a great deal from this same Hodge. I recollect him one day scrambling up Dr Johnson's breast, apparently with much satisfaction, while my friend, smiling and half-whistling, rubbed down his back, and pulled him by the tail; and when I observed he was a fine cat, saying, "Why, yes, Sir, but I have had cats whom I liked better than this"; and then, as if perceiving Hodge to be out of countenance, adding, "But he is a very fine cat, a very fine cat indeed."'

My cats succeed each other in an equality of love – I think. Wintry rifle-shots of frozen branches will honour their graves in the wood.

The question is, will the congregation recognize an Advent sermon that I preached in 1999? Oh, the wickedness of man, who shall know it? Only thou, O God.

The frost delineates the landscape, sharpening it, making the garden tidy. 'We can see where you have been,' say the walkers-by. Where you haven't been, they mean.

I must go to the charity Christmas-card shop without delay; for robins and angels are already flying through the letter box. More importantly – in the long run, that is – I must start to walk the acres that once belonged to my shrunken property, in order to describe them in a new book.

Carrying a Georgian tithe-map, I shall trespass into Duncan-land and Grange-land, Garnons-land, and no-man's-land, and the neighbours will look through their double-glazing and wonder what I am up to. The soil will be cruelly ridged and the puddles frozen. Crump, crump.

But what shivering there is to be done will not be done from the cold this year, but from the Crunch. Whatever happens, it will never be like the farming penury of 1908. A little history, and some faith, could put even this economic tumble into its place, as it were.

Cold-calling on the telephone reaches new heights of impertinence. This week, I have been rung up by the Guild of Will Writers and a moneylender. When I was a child, there were gates that read, 'No Hawkers. No Gypsies'. Theirs was, I recall, a warm-calling of gentle smiles and pleading tongues. There was the Indian with his enormous suitcase filled with silk ties and headscarves which slid on to the doormat. And there were countryfolk for whom the annual round of the higgler was as important as a Feast Day. How else could they get *Old Moore's Almanack* and other necessities?

Cave Canem read some tradesmen's entrances. Sir

Osbert Sitwell declared that when he was walking in Little Venice in London he saw a gate that said, 'Beware of the Doge'. Telephone cold-callers often sound young and desperate, and I answer them kindly. What a job, I tell myself. All that slamming down of receivers, all those hostile voices. Seventh-Day Adventists have given up coming to save me, put off by the muddy track.

Margery Allingham and This Mortal Life

DAWN – my Trappist hour. Tentative light fingers the land. Tom and the others will be bumping along to the station in their second-best cars. Morning television and cereals, school buses, the flock down by the church eating and eating, glinting with frost. Such activity! Though not at Bottengoms Farm, where nothing whatever is heard or done. But staring through a window in winter when there is no sun keeps me on the go.

I am drinking Clipper green tea, and faintly worrying; for William Hazlitt died of green tea, admittedly having drunk 40 cups a day. This box of it tumbled into my possession in the supermarket. It tastes bookish. The white cat comes in from the cold and goes to bed on me, usurping my warmth. The big decision is, shall I dress before breakfast or after? Might I dare to read? or hear the News? or stand up and dislodge a moribund cat? These things have to be considered when one is a writer. It is much easier to commute to the City, or find a fresh bit of grass.

Also, I am haunted by Advent, by its mystery and

grandeur. It was once kept as a less stringent Lent, stern and preparatory. But now, chiefly owing to its marvellous hymns – which we, for some strange reason, now dub 'carols' – it has become a most extraordinary time, one that, though defying analysis, has the power to bring our faith to glorious heights.

Evensong in our country church, with its liturgy and music, plus the profundity of the spaces in between, 'now in the time of this mortal life', as its collect says, did indeed raise us to the comprehension of immortality. Even Amos would have approved. It was very beautiful; the 'dreadful majesty', the 'thrilling voice'. The plaintive petitions. The 40-or-so of us for an hour or so in that other sphere, one whose language has to be relearned or comprehended if we are to get anywhere.

I am having to write an introduction to Margery Allingham's *The Oaken Heart*, published in 1941. She lived a few miles from Wormingford, and belonged to that brilliant group of mid-twentieth-century whodunit women novelists – Dorothy L. Sayers, Agatha Christie, Ngaio Marsh, etc. – who are unsurpassed in this genre.

The Oaken Heart, however, is no mystery. It is rural Essex waiting for Hitler. Allingham wrote it rapidly from her even faster diaries. Here is the Battle of Britain, Dunkirk, the fall of France described without retrospect by a young woman living in a big country house. That she is a novelist is obvious: that she has to work like mad not to turn her neighbours into 'characters' is plain. Yet few Second World War historians or even participants have been able to capture the essence of this moment as she has done. And how rural England has changed! And without invasion. And how she brings out the boredom of war, and all unintentionally. A reprint soon. Watch out.

No cries on market-day. The stallholders are mum. We trudge through their ever-growing ranks until the fish stall brings us to a halt. Who could pass it? It reeks of the North Sea. Our senses swim. From the deep to the deep-freeze. Bitter, bitter cold it is outside.

Waiting

ADVENT SNOW. A white world. Green woodpeckers tug at the chicken fragments left over from the lunch I cooked for the young artist. The cold is amazing. Two-jersey days. You can hear the trees cracking. The unseen hunt howls down in the valley, and geese whirr through the leaden sky. I am burning aspen logs and casting away the works of darkness, of course. Tangible Advent! 'Owe no man anything,' Paul is telling the Romans. 'It is high time to awake out of sleep,' he goes on; 'for now is our salvation nearer than when we believed.'

At evensong, I preach on 'Waiting'. As I light the first 'waiting' candle, one on the altar, caught in a draught, makes a shroud and has to be put out. Such is life. A boy arrives; an old man dies. The boy is adorned with a string of lovely names: Emmanuel, Adonai, Dayspring, Desire of Nations. Who names this Child? The windows are black, the music haunting. Outside, our cars are freezing.

In Advent, it is always like this: both matter-of-fact and profoundly strange. As Paul said, salvation has crept up on us, and we are disturbed. We wait. We wait patiently at the check-out and in the communion queue. The prophet Micah said simply: 'I will wait for God my Saviour.' If we remember that 'advent' stems from the same root as 'adventure' we shall catch its drift.

But the gentle mutual approach between God and man is darkened by Isaiah, who sees a judge inexorably approaching 'to argue his case and to open an indictment against those who have ravaged the vineyard'. Vineyards go to rack and ruin when all our energies are employed elsewhere.

The students are not waiting for the Government's dubious plans for their education. They swarm through the streets. It is almost as good as Paris. The young do not need to be energized: they are fully alive, passionate, and free.

The Department for Education is a mite too slick, and needs to be less glib in its pronouncements. Fast-talking Michael Gove deserves to be overtaken by this torrent of youth, no matter what the deficit. The Lib Dems are bobbing about on it like driftwood. It is worrying and exhilarating at the same time. You can say things at the age of 20 which would not pass your lips at 50; and so you should. It is sad to grow old and to have never rioted. Or just marched. I am sure that Montaigne would have agreed.

No letters these three days. Jamie the postman cannot get down the farm track. It is a kind of bliss. No emails, of course. Rabbit-guards make pencil lines across the snow. Winter wheat lies snug beneath its icy duvet. French partridges run around in family groups. Georgian tombstones, too, are neatly blanketed. Stripped trees rattle in a north wind.

When I shake hands at the church door, I am given every degree of circulation, hot paws, frigid paws, some scrabbling for car keys, others piled with hymn books. Dear, dear old friends, they and I full of holy platitudes and small bursts of concern, and gentle kisses. Our service is done. The December night engulfs us. In churchfield at Wormingford, a hundred or more sheep sleep in woolly humps, cosy in the snow, all grazing done. A brittle hedge keeps them out of the churchyard.

Sound Hilarity

PERCY DEARMER did his best to introduce what he called 'sound hilarity' in church services. He deplored the tackling of difficult anthems by the average church choir, and said that it should sing a carol instead. He and his colleagues Martin Shaw and Ralph Vaughan Williams put together the still-marvellous *Oxford Book of Carols* in 1928, and it continues to make perfect Christmas reading.

I am writing this in a small Tudor farmhouse on the banks of the River Stour, with frosted rosebuds softly knocking against the window and the radio promising more snow. The sound hilarity of centuries of country children has to be imagined, not heard.

The original tenants would have heard the Prayer Book of King Edward VI, a boy. *Cantate Domino* at matins, *Memento, Domine* at evensong – 'I have ordained a lantern for mine Anointed.' And maybe a wax candle or two would have lit the low rooms. Berryless ivy stretches to the sky in the top garden. The oaks look as though they are saying, 'Maybe our leaves will do for another year.'

On Christmas Day in young Edward's Prayer Book they couldn't spell for toffee. 'And straytways there was with the angel a multitude of heavenly souldiers, praisying God, and saying: Glory be to God on hye, and peace on the yearth, and unto men a good wyll.' After which there were 12 days of eating up everything that could not be salted down, preserved, or hung in the chimney. I still have the hooks to prove it. The white cat will swing on them, given a chance.

Myriad church services stretch our charity. My television set has shut down of its own accord, being almost Tudor, and, say my comforters, 'Now you can buy a flat screen!'

The Christmas guests have never had a TV of any kind, humpbacked or flat, and have relied on me to tell them what they have missed. At the moment, however, I revel in the loss. Glorious music is on tap – today, some French nativity music by Charpentier and Saint-Saëns, plaintive and ethereal, tentative and more sky-caught than of the 'yearth'. In church, we sing 'In the bleak midwinter' to Gustav Holst in moderate time, caught at the heart as usual.

Time, and what the brand-new lectionary calls Ordinary Time – something I haven't quite mastered – begin their sacred cycle. Round and round they go, the farm work and the church work, making poetry en route, creating salvation – although not as totally as they once did. It is also the Christmas before the Cuts, and there is an unspoken foreboding. As well as the Saviour, a new politics is being born.

I am feeding green woodpeckers and blackbirds with Waitrose muesli. I ask you! But I seem to have run out of scraps or whatever. They bounce around the feast with glossy breasts. Countless rooks make short work of the horse-feed. As for robins, they are as fat as people. Tamer, too. At night, river owls cry under a quarter moon. Wise mice stay at home.

The river itself is almost still, and I have to gaze hard at its iciness to detect a current. It is like having to feel for a pulse in an arm. Wintertime is surely here. Boots crump on grass. Autocratic riders salute me as they pass. 'Cold, cold,' we say. Winter wheat is as straight as a die. The landscape is all lined up for what is to come. I am nicely freezing under my clothes.

On Christmas Eve, Ian will arrive from the Barbican, and Joachim from Berlin. Joachim will light the dinner-table candles, break a white bread-roll in a snowy napkin, and say the prayers for the evening of the sabbath. Later, he will drive me to the midnight mass at Little Horkesley. Henry, our Vicar, will be assisted by James, the chaplain of Chelmsford Prison. I will administer the cup. Ancient hands, young hands, kneeling forms. Our Saviour, not Joachim's – not yet. He is prayerful every day. He designs gardens, including the garden of the Holocaust Memorial in Berlin. When I hear him reciting the Shabbat psalm I think, 'How could they?'

I think of Joseph, Mary, and Jesus reciting it, careful not to keep the expensive candles burning too long, careful with the words. After the midnight mass, early on Christmas morning, we sit by the dwindling fire and have a whisky; three old friends who write books. It is our December rite from times long past. Habit, pattern, devoted repetition. Different sacraments.

The main difference in an old farm-turned-house is the absence of creatures. A cat excepted. Pigs, horses and cows, chickens and ducks, would have been slumbering only a few yards from where we are still awake. Chomping and rustling, making their presence known. We would have gone around with the lantern to see that they were safe before we went upstairs. There would have been a nice smell of muck, and much breathing. Christmas animals they would have been – we would have told them so.

There were knitted sheep and oxen in the church crib. In the Middle Ages, the crib was placed behind the high altar, and two priests dressed as midwives attended it. People were very practical then. And very agricultural.

Fields and barns, stockyards and pastures, meadows and woods seem to have run into naves and chancels without so much as a by-your-leave. Thomas Hardy saw the hobnailed boots of labourers strike sparks from the gravestones in the aisle on Christmas morning. There was no holiday for them, not even on such a day. Feeding, watering, going round, yet revelling; for:

Herdsmen beheld these angels bright –
To them appeared with great light,
And said, 'God's son is born this night.'

This king is come to save his kind,
In the scripture as we find; –
Therefore this song have we in mind:

Then, dear Lord, for thy great grace,
Grant us the bliss to see thy face,
Where we may sing to thy solace.

This was written in 1456. What language! Sometimes, I fancy I hear it in the farmhouse, used to send the children to sleep or to keep spirituality awake. Hugger-mugger it was then against the cold, the natal music firing the rooms. And there was all that food that wouldn't keep. And tipsy wine from the hedges. And human love and beauty. And devilish aches and pains, since it was winter. And draughts you could cut with a knife. And this little boy.